# ONE BILLION AMERICANS

# ONE BILLION AMERICANS

---

## THE CASE FOR THINKING BIGGER

---

**Matthew Yglesias**

PORTFOLIO ★ PENGUIN

Portfolio / Penguin
An imprint of Penguin Random House LLC
penguinrandomhouse.com

Most Portfolio books are available at a discount when purchased in quantity for sales promotions or corporate use. Special editions, which include personalized covers, excerpts, and corporate imprints, can be created when purchased in large quantities. For more information, please call (212) 572-2232 or email specialmarkets@penguin randomhouse.com. Your local bookstore can also assist with discounted bulk purchases using the Penguin Random House corporate Business-to-Business program. For assistance in locating a participating retailer, email B2B@penguinrandomhouse.com.

LIBRARY OF CONGRESS CATALOGING-IN-PUBLICATION DATA

Names: Yglesias, Matthew, 1981– author.
Title: One billion Americans: the case for thinking bigger / Matthew Yglesias.
Description: New York : Portfolio, 2020. | Includes bibliographical references.
Identifiers: LCCN 2020027461 | ISBN 9780593190210 (hardcover) | ISBN 9780593190227 (ebook)
Subjects: LCSH: United States—Population—Economic aspects. | United States—Population—Environmental aspects. | Demographic transition—Economic aspects—United States. | United States—Emigration and immigration—Government policy. | United States—Economic conditions—21st century.
Classification: LCC HB3505 .Y45 2020 | DDC 304.6/20973—dc23
LC record available at https://lccn.loc.gov/2020027461

Printed in the United States of America
1  3  5  7  9  10  8  6  4  2

Book design by Cassandra Garruzzo

For Kate, my one in a billion

# Contents

# PART III
# We Can Have Nice Things

# Introduction

## America Is Too Small

The American political system has fallen into a state of torpor and dysfunction driven by, among other things, the absence of a shared sense of purpose.

Disagreement and debate are vital in a free society. But it's also useful at times to have common goals—settle the West, beat the Nazis, win the Cold War—that structure the disagreements. What we've been doing lately isn't so much debating how to proceed as a country as it is simply fighting with one another. And now the country faces a very real challenge that we must meet: rapid ongoing economic growth in India and especially China is leading to the relative decline of the United States of America as a great power and threatens its position as the world's number one state in the not-too-distant future.

Contemporary American politicians give no sign of wanting to accept that decline, but they're also not proposing to do anything about it. There's no way that all the specific ideas in this book will ever command broad consensus in American society. But I think the *big picture* idea of the book, that America should try to stay number one, already does. The question is what follows from that.

For starters, it is beyond dispute that there are fewer American people than there are Chinese or Indian people, as is the fact that China and India are trying to become less poor and seem to be succeeding. Maybe they'll just stumble and fail, in which case we will stay number one. But it would be unfortunate for hundreds of millions of people to be consigned to poverty forever. It's not an outcome we have it within our power to guarantee. And even if we could, it would be hideously immoral to pursue it.

By contrast, tripling the nation's population to match the rising Asian powers is something that is in our power to achieve. It would require more immigrants and more programs to support people who want to have additional children. And of course if we had a lot more people, we'd need to adjust a number of other things to make sure they had jobs and places to live. Working out the exact details of how best to structure family support programs, how best to pay for them, exactly which additional immigrants to let in, and how to improve our infrastructure and increase our housing stock are good things to argue about. The ideas laid out in this book are the best ones I could find. But nothing will command universal assent or be beyond the realm of political dispute and political bargaining.

But think of how much healthier our politics would be if there were really a debate about how to accomplish great things rather than a food fight over semi-imagined offenses to "real Americans" that serves as a mask for an endless procession of tax cuts for the rich. Why not make America greater than ever instead?

Conservatives argue that the country is "full" and we can't take more immigrants. Progressives tend to disagree, even while being inclined to say that the particular towns and cities they live in are full and don't need more real estate development. America's birth rate has slipped to historic lows and nobody in the political mainstream seems to think we can or should do anything about it. Meanwhile, the seemingly unstoppable rise of China as a world power hangs like a dark cloud over American politics.

None of this is right.

Early in my career, I focused largely on foreign policy topics. But for more than a decade, I've primarily covered domestic issues. And as I've done so, I've been struck by the growing popularity of the view that somehow foreigners—whether through immigration or trade—are to blame for our various domestic problems.

The truth is exactly the reverse. We didn't prosper in the late twentieth century because we won the Cold War; we won the Cold War because our underlying political and economic system was a lot better than Soviet communism. Today our international situation is imperiled because we have let a staggering array of lingering problems fester and prevent us from becoming as big and as rich a country as we ought to be.

But the United States is not "full." Many of its iconic cities— including not just famous cases of collapse like Detroit but also Philadelphia and Chicago and dozens of smaller cities like Rochester and Erie—actually have fewer residents than they had decades ago. And virtually all of our thriving cities easily have room to grow and accommodate more people.

And we should accommodate more people. Immigrants of virtually all stripes help make native-born Americans richer, make our retirement programs more sustainable, and offer the fuel for innovation that can help the country grow. Housing shortages are endemic in many parts of the country, but the tools to surmount them are easily available and—like immigration—would cost taxpayers nothing. Providing adequately for America's families—by offering not just paid leave but financial assistance, preschool and aftercare services, reasonable summer programming, and affordable college for all qualified students—would cost money. But it would greatly benefit America's children and make it much easier for middle-class people to have the number of kids they say they want.

As a policy reporter, I'm much more a generalist than a specialist. And I like doing stories about solutions. Like many people, when I look at something long enough I start to see patterns in it.

* The solution to America's new urban housing crisis is to build more houses so more people can move to in-demand cities.
* The solution to the illegal immigration crisis is to let more people come legally, not tie ourselves into knots trying to stop the flow.
* Both America's vast rural hinterland and many of its aging northeastern and midwestern cities need an influx of

people to prevent their current priceless assets from wasting away.

* America's families need help from a more robust welfare
state in order to be able to have and raise children with
secure middle-class lifestyles.

But for a long time these patterns seemed to be parts of a puzzle whose pieces didn't quite fit together. More immigration is good, but the cities the immigrants tend to move to already don't have enough housing. More housing is good, but that might only exacerbate rural depopulation. What put it all together was glancing back into the foreign policy realm. What the various diplomats and admirals and trade negotiators and Asia hands who think about the China question don't want to admit is that all the diplomacy and aircraft carriers and shrewd trade tactics in the world aren't going to make a whit of difference if China is just a much bigger and more important country than we are. The original Thirteen Colonies, by the same token, could have made for a nice, quiet, prosperous agricultural nation— like a giant New Zealand. But no number of smart generals could have helped a country like that intervene decisively in World War II.

If sane, humane child and family policy gives us more people; and sane, humane immigration policy also gives us more people; and if declining areas need more people but expensive areas also need more housing, then the solution to the puzzle is that we should do it all and stay number one forever.

A more populous America—filled with more immigrants and more children, with its cities repopulated and its construction industry booming—would not be staring down the barrel of inevitable relative decline. We are richer today than China or India. And while we neither can nor should wish for those countries to stay poor, we can become even richer by becoming larger. And by becoming larger we will also break the dynamic whereby growth in Asia naturally means America's eclipse as the world's leading power.

The United States has been the number one power in the world throughout my entire lifetime and throughout the living memory of essentially everyone on the planet today. The notion that this state of affairs is desirable and ought to persist is one of the least controversial things you could say in American politics today.

We should take that uncontroversial premise seriously, adopt the logical inference that to stay on top we're going to need more people—about a billion people—and then follow that inference to where it leads in terms of immigration, family policy and the welfare state, housing, transportation, and more.

Admittedly, it sounds a little loopy. But while some left-wing intellectuals might suggest that the end of American hegemony would be desirable, I've never heard an elected official from either party articulate that view. The desirability of staying on top is made all the more obvious by the fact that the main rival we face is not something cuddly like a hypothetical version of the European Union (EU), which managed to actually get its act together and coordinate foreign policy.[*]

---

[*]The idea of the EU as a potential geopolitical success story was fashionable in the midaughts, when Iraq brought America low and before the Eurobond crisis and Brexit. Glyn Morgan's book *The Idea of a European Superstate* (Princeton, NJ: Princeton University Press, 2007) is an

Instead, American power is rivaled by the growing power of the People's Republic of China, a country that's aggressively using its commercial clout to try to silence critics abroad, conducting egregious human rights abuses against its Uighur minority, and cracking down on freedoms in Hong Kong.

It would be nice to think that the Chinese will step away from their autocratic political system. It would be nice to think that even if they don't, the US-China relationship will stay friendly. Whether it does or doesn't, the United States will presumably want to try to have close relationships with our traditional allies in the Pacific and ideally make new friends in Vietnam, India, and beyond. Other people have written books about that subject and will continue to write new ones.

This book is about something more basic: the reality that the balance of power is shifting away from America and toward China, and beyond it, India and Nigeria and others. And the reasons for this are not in any way mysterious. When America faced down Nazi Germany and the Soviet Union, we were the big dog.* We had more people, more wealth, and more industrial capacity. But against China we are the little dog: there are more than 1 billion of them to about

---

impressive theoretical argument for the idea that the EU should become a geopolitical player. But events have gone in the other direction.

*There is, of course, a lot more than this to be said about the specific dynamics of World War II and the Cold War, including many fine books on the wartime American economy and Adam Tooze's excellent *The Wages of Destruction* (New York: Viking, 2006) on the detailed operation of the Nazi economy. But in a big picture sense, Paul Kennedy's classic macrohistory *The Rise and Fall of the Great Powers* (New York: Random House, 1987) is chock-full of tables underscoring the basic weight of raw manpower, coal, steel, and iron production in driving the power politics of the nineteenth and twentieth centuries.

330 million of us. The good news is that, for now, we still have more wealth and more industrial capacity because Americans, on average, are about four times as rich as Chinese people.

But that gap in per capita gross domestic product (GDP) is shrinking. It shows every sign that it will likely continue to shrink.

Most fundamental, the only real way for it to stop shrinking would be for China to suffer some horrendous misfortune or for its government to make some tragic miscalculation. This is, of course, not impossible.* But it would be silly to count on it. And while there are reasonable debates to be had about securing our country against industrial espionage and trying to maintain our companies' intellectual property, it's silly to think there's anything we could actually do to keep China poor, and the ethics of trying to pull that off are extremely dubious.

At the same time, while we obviously can and should do what we can to make Americans richer—you'll find ideas about that in here too—there are some profound reasons why it's essentially impossible for a rich country like the United States to grow as rapidly as a still-poor country like China.

The good news is that for all its many flaws, our country has a much healthier political and economic system than China's. Consequently, there is every reason to believe that the average American will enjoy higher material living standards than the average Chinese person.

---

*Argentina, famously, was one of the richest countries in the world at the beginning of World War I, only to stumble into a seemingly endless series of policy errors that have ended with it left in the dust by Japan, Singapore, South Korea, Taiwan, and essentially all of Eastern Europe, to say nothing of the truly rich countries of North America and Western Europe.

But a three-to-one advantage in population is really hard to overcome. Chinese people don't need to become as rich as Americans for China's overall economy to outweigh ours. If they were to manage to become about half as rich as we are on a per person basis, like the Bahamas or Spain, then their economy would be far larger than ours in the aggregate. To become one-third as rich as we are, like Portugal or Greece, would be enough to pull even. The point is that because China is so big, it doesn't need to come close to beating us on a per person basis to beat us overall—a situation very different from what the United States faced vis-à-vis twentieth-century rivals.

It's not exactly clear what would happen if the United States did allow itself to slip to the world's number two economic power. For a while we would almost certainly maintain our global military lead simply because we have so much more experience in global power projection and global alliances. And, obviously, even if China were to become a greater military power, it's not as if we'd have Chinese tanks rolling down the streets of Washington.

But American leaders, with good reason, aren't talking about learning to adapt to a world where the United States is a second-rate power. The problem is that they're also not talking about what it's going to take to avoid that fate. From Barack Obama's rhetoric about the need to "win the future" to Donald Trump's emphasis on tough trade negotiations, politicians from both parties offer theories about how to avoid American decline that are plainly inadequate to the task. China's past thirty years of economic growth have been impressive, but they've also left the People's Republic with roughly the per person income of Mexico. Nobody worries about Mexico dominating twenty-first-century power politics or asks how we're going to stop them from winning the future.

The difference is there are 130 million Mexicans, 330 million Americans, and 1,300 million Chinese people. And to stay on top, we need a *billion* Americans.

That would be, obviously, a large change from the current situation. And to get from here to there would require some large changes in American public policy.

But it's extremely doable. One advantage the United States has over China is that because it is a beacon of freedom to the world rather than an increasingly dystopian oligarchy, there are more than 100 million people who would like to move here than America is prepared to allow in. We shouldn't recklessly throw the borders open to just anyone who happens to show up, but we should recognize that openness to immigration is not just a nice favor the United States does for immigrants. That people want to move here is—and historically has been—a strategic asset, and we have a form of creedal civic nationalism that can accommodate a broad range of newcomers. We should be reasonably selective about whom we let in, but we should let in a lot of people.

I should also note that while reproductive freedom is crucially important, in practice Americans end up having fewer children than they say they would like to have.[*] And it's no great mystery why. Having and raising children is an increasingly costly undertaking,

---

[*]Lyman Stone, "American Women Are Having Fewer Children Than They'd Like," *New York Times*, February 13, 2018.

and the operation of human reproductive biology is a somewhat poor fit for the market economy's increasing tendency to demand that people extend formal education or job training deeper into their twenties.

The idea of taking deliberate action to increase national fertility gives some progressives the willies—just as conservatives are these days in a perennial state of alarm about immigrants—but what's needed isn't some campaign of *Handmaid's Tale* coercion. What American families need is recognition that though the standard K-12 public school concept is invaluable, it's also insanely limited. Children younger than five need to be taken care of, as do children of all ages during the summer months and after 3:30 p.m. Young people increasingly need more education than a high school degree. Providing the public resources necessary to address all these gaps—rather than covering 50 percent of the days for 75 percent of childhood—would be very expensive. But *not* doing it simply pushes the costs onto parents and encourages people not to become parents.

Addressing these concerns would help children and families have healthier, more prosperous lives but also help deliver a healthier, happier country where people are able to have the number of kids they want and American society as a whole is able to thrive for generations to come.

Of course tripling the population could also cause a number of problems. Traffic jams could get worse. Rent could go up. Water access would be stretched thinner. There'd be more pollution. These are, unfortunately, real concerns. But the point of this book is not to try to scare you about China or even to try to convince you that

America should aspire to be the greatest nation on earth. That's what Americans already think and rightly so. What I want to convince you of is that the basic mathematical problem is real, and the various secondary problems that stem from growing the American population are solvable.

Rather than being paralyzed by racial panic, ecopessimism, or paranoia about the loss of parking spaces, we should try to think this stuff through calmly and systematically—choosing to emulate our forefathers and mothers who managed to welcome millions of newcomers and ride oxcarts across the Rocky Mountains to build the greatest nation in human history, rather than throw up our hands at every moderately difficult logistical problem and whine that the country is full.

# PART I

# The Problem

CHAPTER 1

# A Very Short History
# of American Power

The United States of America has been the largest economy in the world since before the development of modern economic statistics during the Great Depression and World War II.[*] But economists and historians have attempted to reconstruct GDP data for the past by using what information is available, and they've generally concluded that aggregate income and output in the United States had already exceeded that of the British Empire by the eve of World War I.[†] At this point, the United States also exceeded England in terms of income per person, and obviously far exceeded the larger British Empire, which at the time included deeply impoverished places like India and a large chunk of Africa.

---

[*]See Diane Coyle, *GDP: A Brief but Affectionate History* (Princeton, NJ: Princeton University Press, 2015), for the development of the economic data we take for granted today.

[†]The standard source is Angus Maddison, *Contours of the World Economy, 1–2030 AD: Essays in Macro-Economic History* (Oxford: Oxford University Press, 2007), table A.4.

That enormous economic might allowed us to intervene decisively in both the First and Second World Wars, in both cases first through our power as a source of agricultural commodities and industrial products and then secondarily as an actual fighting force of soldiers, sailors, and airmen.

Of course we won the war against Nazi Germany and Imperial Japan in no small part thanks to the valor of our troops at war. But on another level, the Axis scarcely had a chance. Back in 1938, the gross domestic product of the United States alone was larger than that of Germany, Japan, and Italy combined.* In practice, of course, the Axis also had to take on the large Soviet Union and the British Empire. But America alone had enough economic mass to take down its rivals. That manifested itself in the United States bringing superior matériel to bear on the battlefield; in American civilians enjoying higher wartime living standards than what was seen on foreign home fronts; and in America's ability to serve as the "arsenal of democracy" (and of Soviet communism), supplying vast quantities of useful material resources to our allies through the Lend-Lease Act.

But Germany was a wealthy, technologically advanced society, and Japan, though poorer, was not exactly an economic slouch. Germany's basic problem was that even after taking over Austria and the Sudetenland, it had only 80 million people. The United States had 130 million.

---

*See Mark Harrison, *The Economics of World War II: An Overview* (Cambridge, UK: Cambridge University Press, 1998), 23–24, for a detailed discussion of these statistics, including nuances to account for German territorial expansion during the first few years of the war.

The Soviet Union, by contrast, consistently maintained a population that was larger than America's. The United States was, however, much richer throughout that entire conflict and consequently was able to mobilize much more national power. The basic closeness of the population dynamics, however, made Cold War competition something akin to a "fair fight." If communism had been a good idea as an economic strategy, the Soviets could have caught us on per capita living standards and exceeded us in total national income and output. Instead, it was a bad idea, and they didn't.

China and India, however, have a lot more people than we do, not a little bit more. And that means good economic policy alone won't be enough to keep us ahead.

Because the point of this book is the proposition that we ought to take decisive steps to avert falling behind China, it's natural for readers to want me to project exactly when China will overtake us under current policies. Once upon a time, I thought this would be a straightforward thing to look up with Google. But it turns out that if you try it, you get a range of different answers. In part that's because, as either Niels Bohr or Yogi Berra or both once quipped, predictions are hard, especially about the future.

But in part it's because the predictors are to an extent talking about different things. That's why one Bloomberg headline from 2018 argued that China had *already* become the world's biggest economy and urged Americans to "get used to it"[*] while one three

---

[*]Noah Smith, "Get Used to It, America: We're No Longer No. 1," *Bloomberg*, December 18, 2018.

months later argued that "extrapolating when the world's second-biggest economy will overtake the first is a tricky business riddled with caveats" and it would perhaps *never* happen.* I don't particularly want to take a side in this international economic statistics nerd fight, but it's also a bad idea to just throw up our hands and say we have no way of knowing.

## How rich is China, really?

One thing that makes comparisons hard is that each country measures its economy in its own currency. To do a comparison, you need to convert into a common currency using exchange rates. According to the International Monetary Fund, for example, in 2018 the per capita GDP in the United States was $62,870 while in Denmark it was $60,900. The United States, in other words, was about 3 percent richer.

Market exchange rates are, however, very volatile. Over the course of July 2019, for example, the value of the British pound fell about 5 percent relative to the value of the US dollar thanks to the growing realization that Boris Johnson was going to become prime minister. That 5 percent decline had some real implications for the living standards of the British people (it was really bad news for anyone who had already booked an August vacation to the United States)

---

*David Fickling, "China Could Outrun the U.S. Next Year. Or Never." *Bloomberg*, March 8, 2019.

and contains serious information about investors' sense of the long-term implications of the situation in British politics. But obviously the typical British person did not suddenly become 5 percent poorer in any meaningful sense over a single month that summer. Financial markets just bounce around much more rapidly than actual economic conditions change.

For countries like China that don't allow their exchange rate to float up and down in the free market, the problem is different. You get a good deal of stability, but you also get changes that happen because of the shifting winds of government policy rather than economic conditions.

International economic organizations try to deal with this reality by using what they call purchasing power parity (PPP). This works when organizations survey the world for what a representative basket of goods and services—tomatoes, haircuts, refrigerators, shoes, pasta, rent—costs in local currency in each country. Then by doing a little mathematical wizardry to account for how important each particular item in the basket is to a typical household, they construct a measure that allows them to say, for example, that Spain's GDP lets them buy about US$40,000 worth of stuff per person while in America we are closer to US$60,000 per person. The PPP adjustment offers stability relative to market exchange rates. It also changes some countries' relative ranks. Denmark and the United States are very similar in GDP per capita at market exchange rates, but with PPPs in place, Denmark looks almost 13 percent poorer than the United States on account of things being more expensive there.

Typically in a poor country you'll find that per capita income looks better with PPP adjustments. Precisely because poor countries are poor, it is cheap to hire people there to do labor-intensive services like cutting hair or cleaning houses.

Because China is a lot poorer than the United States—and because at times its government deliberately undervalues its currency to help export-oriented businesses—the PPP adjustment turns out to make a big difference. So big, in fact, that in PPP-adjusted terms China is already number one.

That said, the statistics themselves are human contrivances. In China's case, contrivances are put together by an authoritarian political system with no free speech, free press, or opposition political party to question the official data. Consequently, almost everyone thinks Chinese economic statistics are somewhat fake.

Wei Chen, Xilu Chen, Chang-Tai Hsieh, and Zheng Song—researchers at the Chinese University of Hong Kong and the University of Chicago—concluded in a blockbuster paper presented at a Brookings Institution conference in 2019 that, in particular, the reason Chinese economic data suggests such a freakishly high level of investment relative to consumption spending is that a lot of the investment is made up.[*] Consequently, they think the Chinese government's official statistics were overstating the country's growth rate by about 1.7 percentage points per year during the 2008–16 period. This aggregates up to the idea that the Chinese economy is about 16 percent smaller in reality on paper.

---

*Wei Chen, Xilu Chen, Chang-Tai Hsieh, and Zheng Song, "A Forensic Examination of China's National Accounts," *Brookings Papers on Economic Activity*, March 2019, www.brookings .edu/bpea-articles/a-forensic-examination-of-chinas-national-accounts.

On the other hand, if you use market exchange rates instead of PPP-adjusted numbers, then the United States is clearly number one. The Bloomberg columnist David Fickling argued for complacency in a column he led with the question "Remember when Japan was going to become the world's biggest economy?"[*]

And it's true that in the past, predictions that the United States would lose its economic preeminence have fallen flat. The obvious difference between Japan and China, however, is that the United States has more than double Japan's population while less than a third of China's. The forecast that Japan would overtake the United States was, in effect, a forecast that Japan would become a much richer country than America, which didn't pan out.

And, indeed, it's extremely foolish to look at the fact that a poorer country is growing faster than the United States and then just draw a line projecting that into the indefinite future. China has been growing faster than the United States for a long time now, but Chinese growth has been slowing and it will almost certainly slow further still long before the average Chinese person is as rich as the average American.

But China doesn't need to catch the United States in per person terms to beat us in the aggregates. Indeed, it doesn't even need to come particularly close. If China is able to replicate the success of Japan, South Korea, Taiwan, or the better off post-communist states of central Europe, that would be good enough.

There are, obviously, no guarantees in life, and predicting the

---

[*]Fickling, "China Could Outrun the U.S. Next Year. Or Never."

future is inherently challenging. But the conventional estimates holding that China's economy will likely overtake the United States sometime in the 2030s or 2040s are well grounded in past experience and don't require any particularly rosy theories about future Chinese prosperity. To get it done, China needs to follow the footsteps of other formerly fast-industrializing Asian powers, not surpass them in some noteworthy way. It's always possible that the Chinese will screw up and it won't happen. But if they *don't* screw up, there's probably not much we can do to stop them from catching up.

## Catching up is (relatively) easy to do

The United Kingdom had the world's first industrial revolution and also its slowest. That's no coincidence. In the initial decades of industrialization, absolutely everything had to be invented anew and deployed for the very first time. New machines were created, and industrialists had to decide whether or not to roll the dice on them. Both supplies of raw materials and consumer markets for the output had to be found. It was difficult, painstaking work, and while industrializing, Britain secured a sustained rate of economic growth that had never before been seen in the world. The actual numbers involved were unimpressive by contemporary standards.

Economic growth in the modern world is still difficult in the sense that many countries struggle to get on the track of industrialization in the first place.

But latecomers to the industrialization game, whether that's southern Europe in the 1950s and 1960s, Japan in the 1970s and 1980s, Korea and Taiwan in the 1990s, or China in the twenty-first century, get to take advantage of what came before them. Machines that have already been perfected can simply move into place in order to feed markets that have already been established. Foreign experts can be hired and a country's own people can train abroad. This is what's called catch-up growth, when a poor country is able to develop very rapidly in part precisely because it is poor.

Some of this is mere copying—the United States, for example, spent the nineteenth century declining to respect English patents and created huge incentives for US-based entrepreneurs to "steal" British technology. But even in more genuinely innovative spaces, latecomers are able to take advantage of the fact that others have already blazed these trails. China, for example, is currently developing a domestically designed single-aisle passenger jet intended to compete with Boeing's 737 and Airbus's A320 aircraft families. This is original work. But the Chinese are in a position to know, broadly speaking, what kinds of airplanes there is a robust market for. They also knew from the start that the 737 wing design, which was originally developed in the 1960s, is too low to the ground for the bigger, more fuel-efficient modern engines that Boeing tried to stick on the 737 MAX with infamous results.

Today's developing countries are aware of what a modern rich country looks like—and they even have the example of past catch-up success stories to look to, whereas the original industrializers were flying blind.

Because the United States is already rich, it has trouble growing quickly, particularly in a sustained way. Like all countries, ours could do things to improve our economic policies and ideally will in fact do those things. But there is not a ton of low-hanging fruit for America—or Canada or Denmark or Japan or any other rich country—to pick compared with what's available to poorer countries. So while continued convergence in per person living standards between the United States and China might not happen, if it doesn't happen, it's likely to be because of Chinese blunders rather than American successes. And while from a standpoint of international competition that might be nice to see, from a humanitarian perspective it would be a disaster. The rapid growth in China over the past generation has been one of the greatest forces for good in human history. The less spectacular growth in India has also been enormously promising, and everyone with a conscience should hope it continues or accelerates.

Wishing for Chinese economic stagnation is not a viable national strategy, and it's not really something we should wish for. Increasing the rate of per capita economic growth in the United States is a great idea. But doing it to the extent necessary to stay number one is extremely unlikely to work. By contrast, our rate of population growth is pretty easy to alter.

## American growth is slowing down

US population growth famously spurted forward in the post–World War II baby boom years before slowing down. What's less well known is that it has continued slowing down ever since and has now reached record lows.

The slowdown in actual birth rates has been even more dramatic because the declining number of babies was partially offset for much of this period by a rising number of immigrants.

But a combination of the Great Recession and the roughly contemporaneous hardening of the US-Mexico border led to a reduction in illegal immigration from Mexico. Then under Trump, the United States began moving to curtail the number of people who move here legally while somewhat increasing the pace with which those present illegally are removed. Trump, of course, wants to enact further sharp reductions in legal immigration, and his view of this has become increasingly mainstream in Republican Party circles.

Conservatives are much more rhetorically favorable toward the idea of people having babies than they are toward immigrants. But in policy terms, the contemporary GOP is essentially bereft of ideas that would actually make it easier for Americans to bear the significant financial costs of raising children, and many of their plans for curtailing the social safety net would have the opposite impact. Democrats are better at talking about child care and preschool costs but have mostly deprioritized family issues in favor of talking about health care.

The result is that the country is currently on course to accept a continued decline in population growth rates. The basic economic pressures that make it increasingly difficult for people to form families aren't going to be ameliorated by magic—on the contrary, they are overwhelmingly likely to accelerate—and the huge wave of illegal immigration from Mexico that powered population growth until ending more than a decade ago isn't going to come back. These are, however, policy choices, not inevitable features of the landscape. What we need to do is make different choices.

A country that did more to support families and welcome immigrants would be a richer, stronger country. And an America on track to grow would be in a position to cooperate, not just compete, with the other major powers.

## A cooperative world

Major countries often compete with one another for power and prestige. But many of the world's biggest problems—from pandemic disease to climate change—can fundamentally be solved only through international cooperation.

And in a way, it's only by recommitting ourselves to winning the competitive aspects of geopolitics that we can succeed at the cooperative ones. Take climate change, where the international aspects pose some of the most profound difficulties—especially because China is the world's largest emitter and India is gaining ground quickly. No one country's efforts to restrain emissions will successfully halt the warming of the planet. But each country is better motivated to take steps toward sustainability if it can be reasonably assured that *all* countries are taking similar steps.

Making that happen is easier said than done.

But one underrated impediment to getting it done is that Chinese policy makers see a "keep China poor" agenda as the hidden hand motivating American demands about trade, about alleged national security risks in Chinese technology companies, and everything else. Environmental policy fell off the agenda entirely in the Trump era, but this was definitely one lens through which it was seen in Beijing during Barack Obama's presidency. And while Democrats and Republicans continue to argue vociferously among themselves about climate change, there is now increasing bipartisan skepticism about China on a variety of fronts—and a parallel rising suspicion of American intentions in China.

My experience in reporting on politicians in Washington, DC, tells me that American policy makers regard this attitude as paranoid, and they certainly don't have any explicit plan to try to impoverish China.

But what's also true is that American officials have no explicit plan to embrace the idea of national decline either. And they certainly don't have a plan to match China in population. Under the circumstances, China staying poor is the only way for America to stay on top, and it's natural for Chinese officials to have some concerns about that.

The *One Billion Americans* agenda is in part about competition with the great population centers of Asia. But on another level it's a framework for cooperation with them.

A growing America is an America that controls its own destiny and can secure its own interests without hoping that growth agendas in the developing world stall out and fail. With a rapidly growing population, American officials could say frankly, sincerely, and credibly that we wish the Chinese and others well and hope they can improve the lives of their people as much as possible. Our interest in managing the global commons is what it is—a genuine concern for environmental stability that has nothing to do with worldwide power politics—because we are staying on top no matter how well foreign states do.

The United States is not a meek country nor is it likely to become one. But during the past twenty years we have increasingly become an aggressive country, mired in multiple foreign military conflicts and suffering deteriorating relations with most of the world's other major countries. The *One Billion Americans* agenda is about returning to America's geopolitical posture at its best, not domineering but *self-confident* that our country is secure and strong and that our economic and social system is in fact superior and will be adopted at the end.

We just need to get bigger, which we can easily do—there's plenty of space.

## CHAPTER 2

# America Is Empty

The *One Billion Americans* agenda—tripling the American population—is a radical suggestion that lies well outside the boundaries of conventional political arguments.

But there's nothing radical at all about the basic proposition that a country as large as the United States could fit a billion people into it. China and India each has more than a billion people and less land than the United States.

Right now the United States has about 93 people per square mile. If the aggregate population tripled, then density would too. Many, many countries are far denser than this, including not just city-states like Singapore (more than 20,000 per square mile) or small island nations like Malta (3,913 per square mile) but also poor and arguably "overpopulated" countries like Burundi (1,127 per square mile). Successful developed countries that include a healthy mix of cities, suburbs, and countryside manage to far exceed tripling

America's population density. South Korea has 1,337 people per square mile and Belgium has 976.

The United States contains a significant mountainous region that is not well suited to large-scale habitation. But Japan (899 per square mile) and Switzerland (566 per square mile) have plenty of mountains too.

Another objection is that Alaska accounts for a large chunk of America's land area. This is somewhat less true in reality than a Mercator projection makes it look, but it is true that all the arctic nations—Russia, Canada, Norway, Sweden, Finland—tend toward low population densities.* On a warming planet this is perhaps less of an inevitability going forward than it has been in the past. But I don't want you to think that the viability of one billion Americans hinges on a mass migration to Alaska.

The fact is that even without Alaska, Hawaii, and other overseas territories, the contiguous 48 states are not particularly dense. With about 105 people per square mile, the population of the Lower 48 even when tripled would leave the main part of America about as dense as France and less than half as dense as Germany.

So when you picture a land of one billion Americans, don't imagine an endless sea of gleaming skyscrapers or a vast horrendous slum. Imagine France.

France is a country that does contain gleaming skyscrapers (primarily in the Paris suburb of La Défense) and, unfortunately, a few

---

*Phil Edwards, "Gerardus Mercator revolutionized mapmaking. He was almost executed for it." *Vox*, March 5, 2015, www.vox.com/2015/3/5/8151303/gerardus-mercator-maps.

slums. But it's also the country of the scenic Pyrenees mountains, iconic vineyards, and the rugged coastline of Brittany.

A country of one billion Americans wouldn't look exactly like France any more than Paris looks like an American city. In particular, the New York metropolitan area is already significantly more populous than Greater Paris and under reasonable policy changes several other US cities likely would be too. But nobody thinks of France as a country suffering from a hideous level of overcrowding in part because Denmark, Italy, Germany, the United Kingdom, and the Netherlands are all denser.

This is the key insight that makes the idea of one billion Americans start to go from fantastical to plausible. To get there would require a number of changes, some of them discomforting. But the outcome we are talking about is extremely reasonable—not a transformation of the United States into a continent-straddling version of the Kowloon Walled City or even anything in the neighborhood of the density of East Asian countries like Japan and South Korea. To have one billion Americans, we need to transform the forty-eight contiguous states from being dramatically less dense than Western European countries to being only moderately less dense than they are.

And that's explicitly not including Hawaii and Alaska, primarily because I don't want to be accused of trying to pull wool over the eyes of people by relying on tundra and wildlife preserves to make the idea seem realistic.

But it's not unusual for even fairly crowded countries to have a big empty part somewhere.

The United Kingdom, for example, has a bit more than 700 people per square mile—more than sixfold the population of the Lower 48. But about a third of that British land is Scotland, which, though very beautiful, is also extremely empty. England proper has more than 1,100 people per square mile. For the Lower 48 to become that dense we would need to have 3.5 billion Americans, which is fun to think about but far exceeds any reasonable forecast of how many people would like to move here or what a better family policy could accomplish.

A billion Americans won't turn the country into an overcrowded wasteland; it will be like France—less packed than Germany or Italy. It won't be nearly as dense as the United Kingdom, and we almost certainly couldn't become as dense as England no matter how hard we tried. Like any patriotic American, I have my doubts about all those countries (some don't put enough ice in their drinks, and some have weird ventless dryers that don't actually dry clothing), but they're all perfectly pleasant places that people from all over the world visit happily.

One billion Americans won't make us overcrowded; we're extremely undercrowded today—and significant parts of the country are depopulating.

## The long shadow of the Malthusian past

Thomas Malthus, one of the earliest economists, famously argued that human societies would inevitably become poorer as they become more populated. Eventually a people would become so impoverished that famine or disease would cull the population and lead to a higher standing of living.*

Malthus wrote in the late eighteenth century, on the verge of the Industrial Revolution and the beginning of a long technological liftoff that would prove him wrong. But contemporary economic historians emphasize that Malthus was essentially correct in his understanding of the evolution of living standards up to that point in time. Gregory Clark, a University of California, Davis, economic historian, observes that "even taking one of the richest societies in the world in 1800, England, there is no systematic sign that average incomes had risen beyond the Stone Age."† Which is not to say that there were no differences in living standards over time. There was just no systematic trend toward progress because the key variable was the availability of land.

This is why, somewhat counterintuitively, for the bulk of human history "primitive" hunter-gatherer societies enjoyed higher average living standards than settled agricultural ones.

Hunter-gatherers ate more varied diets, worked fewer hours per year, and as a result of more access to meat and fresh fruit and vegetables, they grew to taller heights and suffered from fewer dental problems and other ailments. Jared Diamond, the celebrated anthropologist and historian, famously dubbed agriculture "the worst

---

*Thomas Robert Malthus, *An Essay on the Principle of Population* (London: T. Johnson, 1798).

†Gregory Clark, "In Defense of the Malthusian Interpretation of History," *European Review of Economic History*, February 2008. See also Gregory Clark, *A Farewell to Alms* (Princeton, NJ: Princeton University Press, 2007).

mistake in the history of the human race."[*] But the "problem" with the hunter-gatherer lifestyle, such as it was, is that it's a very inefficient use of land compared to having peasants settle and cultivate staple crops like wheat, rice, and barley. Grain-oriented agriculture supported higher population densities, which meant bigger armies, which means agricultural societies tended to win in military conflicts with hunter-gatherers. Larger empires and denser populations also led to higher living standards for governing elites, who could skim a much bigger surplus—especially when agriculture was oriented toward commodity grains that are relatively easy to store and transport.[†]

Over time, technological progress also meant improved living standards for elites. But for common people, the effect of progress was inevitably eroded by the impact of population growth. Consequently, a cataclysmic event like the Black Death would lead to a rise in wages because it created a temporary abundance of land.[‡]

This really is how life worked for hundreds if not thousands of years of human history. So it's not surprising that Malthusian presumptions are deeply embedded in our habits of mind. It's natural to think of a more crowded country as necessarily being a poorer one. But the modern economy is different.

---

[*]Jared Diamond, "The Worst Mistake in the History of the Human Race," *Discover*, May 1, 1999, www.discovermagazine.com/planet-earth/the-worst-mistake-in-the-history-of-the-human-race.

[†]James C. Scott, *Against the Grain: A Deep History of the Earliest States* (New Haven, London: Yale University Press, 2017).

[‡]Federal Reserve Bank of St. Louis, "The Black Death in the Malthusian Economy," *The FRED Blog*, December 3, 2018, https://fredblog.stlouisfed.org/2018/12/the-black-death-in-the-malthusian-economy.

## People-powered economies

If you go out to eat in a small town that has only one restaurant, it's unlikely to be very good.

Not because people who live in small towns don't appreciate good food or can't master cooking but because the basic economics of the situation make it challenging. Without many potential customers, a restaurant needs to try to be a "something for everyone" kind of place that caters to all kinds of tastes rather than focusing on anything in particular. There are lots of restaurants like that in big cities and major suburbs too, but they're just uniformly not very good because fundamentally the business model is being broadly acceptable rather than excellent. But in a town with few residents that's essentially the only model that works.

If the town triples in size and supports three restaurants, the situation starts looking more promising. Suddenly it makes sense for one or two of the restaurants to specialize a bit more. If you go up to thirty restaurants, not only do you get specialization, you get competition— two different burger joints offering a slightly different approach.

A larger dining scene also means a deeper labor market. If there are lots of restaurants, then naturally there will be job openings throughout the industry and a real incentive for cooks to try to master their craft and obtain upward mobility. And these positive impacts continue further and further up the scale. A bigger city will have a larger number of more specialized suppliers for restaurants, making it easier for chefs to ply their craft. It will also develop secondary industries like food critics who can hype up the best restaurants and help ensure that investment in quality is rewarded.

And then, of course, there's the human element. Precisely because larger communities are more supportive of a high-quality restaurant industry, the most skilled and ambitious aspiring cooks are likely to move to them. And when they start work, they will have higher-quality peers to learn from and operate in a more competitive marketplace where there is more incentive to improve.

It does remain the case, of course, that natural resources are a source of wealth and that natural resource wealth goes further when it's shared with fewer people. Alaska and California produce approximately the same amount of oil per year, but Alaskans get a lot more out of it with taxes and royalties from oil extraction contributing three to four times as much to the state budget as all other taxes combined.[*] Over and above its direct contribution to the state budget, oil seeded the Alaska Permanent Fund, an investment vehicle that pays out about $1,600 (the exact amount varies per year based on oil prices and other considerations) per person per year.[†]

California, with a population more than fifty times larger than Alaska's, does not reap comparable material rewards from its oil wealth—paying no dividend to citizens and relying overwhelmingly on normal income and sales taxes to finance its government.

---

[*]James Brooks, "Permanent Fund revenue tops oil and taxes as Alaska's budget foundation," *Anchorage Daily News*, March 18, 2019, www.adn.com/politics/alaska-legislature/2019/03/19/permanent-fund-revenue-tops-oil-and-taxes-as-alaskas-budget-foundation.

[†]Gilbert Cordova, "2019 PFD amount officially announced at $1,606," KTUU, September 27, 2019, www.ktuu.com/content/news/2019-PFD-amount-announced-by-the-Department-of-Revenue-561544941.html.

But for its trouble, California has by far the more dynamic economy—hosting four of the world's ten most valuable companies, as well as much of America's start-up scene and cultural exports. Natural resources just aren't that big a deal in the modern economy. However, the threat of infectious disease is a constant reminder that society is built on a biological foundation.

## The specter of disease

The COVID-19 pandemic that burst out of China in 2020 hit New York City extremely hard and extremely quickly. Many wealthy New Yorkers fled to their second homes in the suburbs or to vacation destinations throughout the East Coast. The basic pattern of elites departing disease-ravaged cities for country strongholds is familiar from plague outbreaks in early modern Europe and cholera in the nineteenth century, and reflects the reality that throughout history there has been a tension between the economic opportunities presented by city living and the vulnerability to disease induced by crowding.

That said, there is some reason to doubt the cogency of the link between density and disease vulnerability in the specific case of COVID-19. America's second-densest city, San Francisco, wasn't even close to being the second-hardest-hit city. Both San Francisco mayor London Breed and California governor Gavin Newsom were quick to issue social distancing orders in mid-March, while New York City mayor Bill de Blasio was slower to take equally robust action and

New York governor Andrew Cuomo stepped in as the main leader of the response only once the situation was already out of control.

Under the circumstances, the focus on density looks suspiciously like an effort to deflect attention from policy failures rather than a real diagnosis of the situation. That's especially true because the places generally cited as having the strongest coronavirus responses are generally the developed Asian countries—especially Hong Kong, Singapore, South Korea, and Taiwan—all of which are more than ten times as dense as the United States.

As of this writing, experts continue to disagree as to exactly what the key to Asian success at containment is. But on a broad sociological level it seems clear that jurisdictions that had more experience with SARS earlier in the twenty-first century did a better job at managing the less deadly but harder-to-track COVID-19 outbreak.

That's consistent with the broad historical trend. No society has ever grown and prospered by reacting to infectious disease by abandoning metropolitan living. Successful countries learn how to adopt better public health policies so that life can go on. And while the future of this particular virus remains difficult to predict, it's easy to see that over the long haul, infectious diseases have become less rather than more threatening thanks to the progress of medical science.

Last but by no means least, it's worth recalling that major global cities like New York, Milan, and Paris were joined as early COVID-19 hotspots by tourism hubs like New Orleans and a number of small ski towns in both the United States and Europe. What these places have in common is not density but that they are destinations of a lot of international travel.

Being a place that people want to go to unquestionably poses some public health risks, especially in the opening phase of a brand-new outbreak.

But on another level that's the whole point. There have always been obvious practical downsides to grouping large numbers of people together. We keep doing it, however, because populated places are successful, not despite the other people who are there but because of them.

## Why we cluster

An aspiring actor wants to live in a city where there are plenty of auditions for parts in movies and television shows.

And a long time ago in the early days of the movie industry it was considered economically useful to shoot movies in a place where it was routinely sunny, so it would be easy to get well-lit scenes. So movie studios started operating in Southern California and actors started living there too. The presence of movie professionals made that a logical place to shoot television shows. And even as the actual filming of movies came to be more footloose and involve more location work, the production constraints of television incentivized further clustering. It's good to be filming in a place where there's a ready supply of actors to audition for guest parts.

And it's not just actors. Making movies and TV shows requires specialized tradespeople who know how to do the makeup, design the sets and costumes, and operate the equipment. The industry needs lawyers and accountants just like any other industry, but there are particular quirks to the entertainment world that Los Angeles–based professionals specialize in.

In the modern day, much of this secondary work can be done remotely. A screenwriter, his agent, and the producer to whom they're trying to sell a script could all live in three different cities and conduct their business without ever meeting in person. But in practice, human beings enjoy face-to-face interaction (there's a reason every town of any size has a yoga studio even though you can do yoga at home alone watching videos or using any number of apps) and it's hard to do business deals without face-to-face meetings. You don't *have* to live in Los Angeles to have those meetings (my father is a screenwriter who lives in New York and travels to Southern California every once in a while for meetings), but it's more convenient if you do.

But the other reason why it's good to live in a cluster is what economists call information externalities and normal people might instead call gossip. As the great nineteenth-century economist Alfred Marshall wrote, in an industry cluster "the mysteries of the trade become no mysteries, but are as it were in the air."*

People who work in related fields at different companies talk to one another informally, and information spreads. Teenagers learn the rudiments of the dominate local business from talking to adults in their community, and even people who aren't directly involved in the local specialty become at least broadly conversant with many of its key aspects. That allows know-how and productivity to spread.

*Alfred Marshall, *Principles of Economics* (London: Macmillan, 1890), chapter 10.

But it's also good for building more sophisticated labor markets. The conversations I had with Ezra Klein that led to the cofounding of *Vox* occurred originally in social settings. And while some of our fantastic initial hires resulted from résumés that came in over the transom, many were people whom we knew personally or were recommended by friends—sometimes extremely talented people not currently working in journalism but who had the right skill set and who were persuaded to join us. That worked only because there are lots of journalists living in Washington, especially journalists who cover politics and policy, and there are lots of *other* people who live in DC who aren't journalists but who follow political journalism closely.

What's most important, however, is that even in Washington most people don't work in politics. Nor do most people in the Bay Area or Seattle work in technology. But these successful industry clusters are the modern-day sources of wealth rather than land or natural resources. And while most people don't necessarily work in these industries, what they do is work providing services to other people. Consequently, in the modern world large populations make opportunity more abundant rather than spreading it thinner.

## Doing things for each other

Productivity is the fundamental engine of prosperity. Americans today are much richer on average than the Americans of a hundred years ago (or the Argentines or Angolans of today) because our workers are more productive—we generate more dollars of economic activity per hour of work.

Used in ordinary language, the term productivity sounds like a close analogy of the concept of hard work. But in economic terms, how productive a worker is generally has very little to do with his effort level. Peasants working in rice paddies are working incredibly hard—doing a tremendous number of hours per year of backbreaking labor—but their productivity is extremely low. In fact, on one level they work so hard precisely because the productivity of what they are doing is low. The only way to make a living as a rice farmer with a small plot of land is to work incredibly hard at it.

A person digging gold out of the ground with primitive tools is doing basically the same work as a person digging coal out of the ground. But the gold digger is more productive in an economic sense because gold is more valuable than coal.

In the manufacturing sector, productivity is largely a function of how good the factory's equipment is, whether or not the workers are skilled enough to operate it properly, and how complicated the underlying product is. Textile manufacturing is the paradigmatic low-productivity, low-paying form of manufacturing because making clothing is fairly simple and the machines workers need to do it are cheap and widely available. Workers in a heavily automated car factory, by contrast, are making a complicated and expensive product and using extremely sophisticated machinery to help them do it.

But today most people don't work in farms, mines, or factories. They work in schools, hospitals, restaurants, stores, bars, yoga studios, and salons. And the "fertile land" that people in these lines of work need is access to other people.

Productivity, in the context of in-person services, is in part a function of skill. A surgeon has rarer and more valuable skills than someone who cuts hair. A restaurant chef has more valuable skills than someone flipping burgers at a fast-food restaurant.

But there is also an important dimension of specialization that is fundamentally driven by density. A barista at Starbucks is doing more or less the same job as a barista at Peet's. But the coffee is somewhat different at each chain. And the nature of life is that some people will like one chain's coffee more than the other. A neighborhood that's dense enough to support two different national chain coffee shops will generate better matches between customers and coffee, thus making the workers more productive.

This seems like a trivial thing, but the underlying logic is extremely powerful. Consumers' tastes, needs, and desired trade-offs vary sometimes in arbitrary ways. Providers' skills and interests also vary. And most companies and individual service providers find it easier to do an excellent job when they are able to specialize.

When I was young and broke, I got the cheapest haircuts I could find. Later, older and vainer and more prosperous, I switched to a high-end barber shop that opened in my neighborhood (I'm bald now, but that's a different story). The woman who cut my hair there told me she'd moved from Baltimore because Charm City didn't have enough demand for upscale men's haircuts. There she'd either need to do cheaper cuts, or else work with women's hair, which for whatever reason she didn't want to do. The bigger city made her a more productive worker not because of any magic but because it was large enough to let her specialize in what she wanted to do.

It's well understood that when it comes to physical goods and commodities the ability to trade across international boundaries raises productivity by allowing for more choice, more competition, and more specialization. But in the contemporary world the vast majority of the population works providing locally based services that don't travel very far. The same dynamic of more choice, more competition, and more specialization still drives more productivity and higher living standards, but to achieve it what you essentially need are bigger groups of people.

People sometimes suspect that the higher wages earned in big metropolitan areas are purely a kind of selection effect—the most talented and ambitious people are most likely to move there. There is probably some of this, but two economists, Lionel Fontagné and Gianluca Santoni, studied this in some detail and concluded that the key issue is that "denser commuting zones seem to offer a better match between employers and employees."[*]

When there's a lot of stuff around, it's easier to match workers, customers, and businesses in ways that let everyone do their most valuable work. That's not to say everyone needs to go rush and move to a big city or its suburbs—there are plenty of perfectly good reasons people have to prefer other places to live. But the high productivity

---

*Lionel Fontagné and Gianluca Santoni, "Why denser areas are more productive," *VoxEU*, November 20, 2016, https://voxeu.org/article/why-denser-areas-are-more-productive.

of denser places is good reason to think that a more populous America would be richer rather than poorer. In part because just as rich farmland is beneficial to people who live in cities as well as to farmers, those big dense cities are beneficial even to people who don't live in them.

## The innovation economy

In the short term, lots of different kinds of changes can raise living standards. But in the longer term, what it takes is innovation, or, if you find that to be an annoying contemporary buzzword, *new inventions*.

Today little kids can do video calls with their grandparents across the country, and white-collar workers can be sent home en masse to do their work remotely on Slack and Zoom. Middle-class people can generally afford the occasional plane ticket. Safe, user-friendly electric pressure cookers can turn tough cuts of beef into delicious, tender chili in an hour. Two hundred years ago, by contrast, there was no electricity and consequently no appliances to help relieve the drudgery of domestic tasks. There were no cars, no planes, and in general no faster way to travel long distances than by sailboat. Today we have pills that can treat depression reasonably reliably. Not so long ago we had no antibiotics, and routine infections could easily become fatal illnesses.

It takes more than new inventions alone to raise living standards, but over the long sweep of history they are critical to getting the job done.

And places with more people in them are likely to lead to more invention. This works on a number of levels. One of them is that, as Steven Johnson writes in his book *Where Good Ideas Come From,* cities "are environments that are ripe for exaptation," by which he means that an idea that's in use in one context can be adapted for a new purpose elsewhere.[*]

This is more likely to happen when you have more kinds of people in reasonable proximity to one another. And this in turn reflects the fact that agglomeration benefits are unusually strong in knowledge-intensive industries because ideas spread through informal channels.

Jaison Abel, Ishita Dey, and Todd Gabe (economists with the Federal Reserve Bank of New York, the University of Georgia, and the University of Maine, respectively) examined this in detail in a 2011 paper that paired measures of output per worker in different American metro areas with specific information about the spatial distribution of the population. They found that productivity is higher in denser metro areas, with the effect larger in places where there are more college graduates, and that "these patterns are particularly pronounced in industries where the exchange of information and sharing of ideas are important parts of the production process."[†]

The great thing about innovation is that to an extent everyone

[*]Steven Johnson, *Where Good Ideas Come From: The Natural History of Innovation* (New York: Riverhead Books, 2010).

[†]Jaison R. Abel, Ishita Dey, and Todd M. Gabe, "Productivity and the Density of Human Capital," *Journal of Regional Science,* December 18, 2011, https://onlinelibrary.wiley.com/doi/full/10.1111/j.1467-9787.2011.00742.x.

benefits from it. You don't need to be Swedish to enjoy Spotify or American to enjoy your iPhone.

But, obviously, one major reason that Sweden and the United States are richer than Portugal and Mexico is that they host the headquarters of world-leading companies like Spotify and Apple. This is one of several reasons that it's incredibly foolish of the United States to be squandering the chance to recruit as many smart, skilled immigrants to our shores as we possibly can. Not only will more smart people naturally lead to more great inventions, a greater density of smart people increases the odds that native-born people will innovate. And there is some reason to believe that this could be an especially powerful lever as the country becomes more diverse.

## The power of role models

Given the central importance of inventions and innovations in economic growth, there has historically been surprisingly little work directly examining where it comes from.

But the researchers of the Equality of Opportunity Project have been able to combine a number of different data sets in a unique way to discover something interesting.*

Traditional sources of data on innovation—mostly patents—don't offer much meaningful information on who is doing the inventing,

---

*Alex Bell et al., "Who Becomes an Inventor in America? The Importance of Exposure to Innovation," National Bureau of Economic Research working paper no. 24062, revised January 2019, https://www.nber.org/papers/w24062.

not even including cursory information about the inventor's age and gender. But by linking patent application data from 1996 through 2014 to federal income tax returns, the team was able to track inventors' lives from birth through adulthood to understand who is inventing things and where they come from. And by focusing on the geography of innovation, they have shown that direct exposure to a culture of invention and to role models appears to be playing a key role.

* Among affluent families, young kids who perform highly on math tests are much more likely to make successful inventions than low-scoring kids.
* But this isn't true among low-income families. There, high-scoring and low-scoring kids alike are about equally unlikely to become inventors—suggesting that it isn't a lack of aptitude that's holding back poor kids; it's that aptitude alone isn't enough.
* Kids are more likely to grow up to be inventors when they grow up in cities with other inventors, which means where you're born has a lot to do with whether you'll innovate.
* This holds up even when we look into specific categories of invention. If you grow up in a city full of antenna innovators, you are more likely to innovate regarding antennas—suggesting that early life exposure to relevant networks is important.
* The effect is gender specific—girls are likely to grow up to be innovators only if their city includes an existing

stockpile of female innovators (and similarly, if there are
male role models for boys), underscoring the importance
of role models and self-image.

Particularly fascinating: The geographical aspects hold regardless of where you live as an adult. The Boston area has thriving industrial clusters in both information technology and medical devices. But Boston-area patent holders who grew up in Silicon Valley are very likely to have computer-related patents, whereas those who grew up in Minneapolis, where there's a robust medical device industry, are likely to have medical device patents. In other words, it's not just that people are likely to work in locally thriving industries— the specifics of childhood experience seem to matter.

The implication is that bringing more inventors into the country wouldn't just improve their own productivity (thanks to the great opportunities the United States has long provided to immigrants) but also that of the native-born adults they work alongside (because denser cities are more productive). Potentially it could also inspire more members of the next generation to pursue careers in inventing. Obviously, to deliver maximum effect we need skilled immigrants to live in parts of the country that aren't currently big hubs of immigration. But this is not difficult to manage. Part of what should make immigration a powerful lever for national betterment would be the use of the incredibly large benefits of immigration to shape the terms under which immigrants arrive.

And beyond localized benefits, there are also big national economic benefits to becoming a larger country.

## Home market privilege

When the Trump administration was renegotiating NAFTA, they got the Canadian government to agree to open up to more imports of American dairy products without offering much of anything in return. What the Canadians got was simply that Trump agreed not to follow through on his threats to blow up the whole thing.

And the reason that worked is that even though free trade between the United States and Canada is on average beneficial to both countries, it's more beneficial to Canada—they need us more than we need them.

That's basically just because the United States is so much larger than Canada. American multinationals don't want to lose the Canadian market, but Canadian companies *really* don't want to lose the much larger American market. This isn't a particularly fair situation, and to an extent it reflects Trump's bullying temperament that he so flagrantly took advantage of it. But it's also a fact of life. Bigger economies have an easier time getting their way in international negotiations, and that tends to make them even bigger.

Dairy farmers in Wisconsin and Vermont may not believe they have much in common with people living in New York, Los Angeles, Chicago, Dallas, and Houston, but it's the enormous scale of urban America that helped them batter their way into the Canadian market.

For similar reasons, the large size of the American domestic market makes us a regulatory superpower. Small countries need to take the world as they find it, but if the United States wants to require new safety features on cars or environmental features on dishwashers, then manufacturers will comply rather than risk losing access. Americans take this for granted—we debate the wisdom of various regulatory measures but not their basic feasibility—but this is a privilege stemming from our large size. A smaller country runs the risk of being abandoned by producers if it breaks from the pack.

By the same token, new inventions and new ideas come to our shores quickly because our market is so lucrative. Being big has historically kept the United States on the cutting edge, and getting bigger will serve to do so in the future. And, critically, these and other kinds of benefits extend to Americans living in all kinds of communities.

## Small towns in a big country

In a sense, the benefits of a larger population and more density tend to be found in big cities—the places that have large, dense populations.

But despite its attractions, city living also has a number of downsides, and smaller towns and rural areas have their own considerable appeal. Because the United States is an extremely large country, even in its denser future a great number of people will live in those smaller communities. But there are important economic linkages between city and country that align their interests.

Big metropolitan areas tend to generate higher productivity and income, which is one reason a state like Maine, which doesn't have any of those large cities, tends to be poorer than average. But Mainers still derive considerable wealth and income from the fact that the United States as a whole does have big cities. As is typical of rural communities, Maine exports large quantities of primary commodities— most notably potatoes, lumber, lobsters, and farm-raised salmon and other seafood products. There are international markets for these products (indeed in recent years Maine has started doing a brisk business exporting baby eels to East Asia),* but shipping logistics, tariff barriers, language barriers, and exchange rate uncertainty inherently make it easier to trade closer to home.

American politics, like the politics of most other developed countries, increasingly exhibits polarization along urban-rural lines characterized by intense and bitter culture wars.

On a practical level, however, whether or not people in rural Maine *like* people who live in Boston or New York, their fates are interconnected. That's where the lobster and timber go, and it's where the tourists come from. City dwellers would, obviously, starve and freeze without rural products to consume. And the countryside would be broke without urban markets. Bigger richer cities will mean more prosperous rural areas and small towns as well. Getting Americans to see ourselves as a single national community rather than warring tribes divided by the critical issue of who drives a Prius and who drives an F-150 can feel impossible at times. But the fact is our fates are distinctly linked, both on the level of international competition and economic growth.

---

*Chris Chase, "Maine Elver Season Gets Slower Start, But Values Still Above Average," *SeafoodSource*, April 5, 2019, www.seafoodsource.com/news/supply-trade/maine-elver-season-gets -slower-start-but-values-still-above-average.

A bigger country will be a richer country, and that will be good for everyone. Especially because these days the biggest threats to rural lifestyles are aging and decay.

# The vanishing countryside

Most Americans live in and around the suburbs of big cities, but most of America's land mass comprises small towns and rural areas. And while the rural West continues to add people, most of the land in the United States is currently experiencing population loss.

This somewhat shocking fact has not attracted as much public commentary as it should, but broader questions about the economic problems facing rural communities have.

The specific issues, however, are inextricably linked to the larger phenomenon of population decline.

To be grossly simplistic about it, the basic problem of rural economics is that there are lots of services that are not economically efficient to provide in places where very few people live. Stringing broadband internet wires or constructing cell phone towers is about as expensive in a vast tract of rural land as it is in a normal suburb. But in the suburbs, that cell tower will serve a lot of customers, whereas in a rural area it will serve only a few. Consequently, the rural area is a low priority for business investment. So it tends to end up behind the curve technologically while also facing relatively low levels of competition.

The same is true, unfortunately, for health care. If there is a large population within a given hundred-mile radius, then it can support multiple hospitals to compete with one another and provide a full suite of specialist services. But if there are few people around, the community will be lucky if it supports one hospital and it will be able to employ only a smaller number of medical professionals who are less specialized in their work. Due to both the lack of competition and the small addressable market, that hospital will—like a monopolist internet provider—be relatively sluggish about investing in the newest technologies as well.

Providing low-quality services at a high cost tends to discourage people from living in rural areas. Thus is born a cycle of decline that, like its urban and suburban counterparts, is at least moderately difficult to break.

There are, of course, plenty of ways to address these specific challenges. Making daily mail deliveries to rural areas is cost-ineffective for basically the same reason that it is cost-ineffective to provide them with high-quality mobile phone service. In 1893, Congress appropriated $10,000 for rural free delivery, which, after several years of experimentation and political controversy, was finally expanded, in 1902, into a permanent nationwide service with a large budget.*

Electrical utilities didn't want to invest in serving rural customers for basically the same reasons that broadband providers don't today. The New Deal solved this problem by having the government shoulder the financial burden of making it happen.

---

*"About Rural Free Delivery," United States Postal Service, 2006, https://about.usps.com /publications/pub100/pub100_020.htm.

We could—and probably should—simply pony up the money needed to provide modern communications and health-care services in rural America.

But fundamentally those historical antecedents aimed not just to prop up rural communities with subsidies but to lay the foundation for growth and prosperity. What we need is a virtuous cycle where more public provision of the basics creates more opportunities for people to live and thrive in small-town America, which, in turn, would set off a virtuous cycle of secondary job creation and sustainable public services. The current national population growth aggregates, however, don't support that scenario—especially when you consider that the aging American population is slowing its growth.

About half of America's counties are losing people and a large majority of them are losing prime-age workers.

But while this is a serious economic development for rural America, it's also an opportunity from the standpoint of overall national growth. The United States would benefit, in terms of geopolitical competition, from a more rapid rate of population growth. And it not only has lots of land that *could* accommodate more people, it has lots of land that would *clearly benefit* from more inhabitants.

## The climate can handle more people

Even if America has enough space for hundreds of millions of more people, it's reasonable to worry that the atmosphere can't handle the extra carbon dioxide emissions. The United States has some of the highest per capita emissions in the world, so more Americans equals more emissions, which is bad.

But fundamentally this is too limited a way of looking at the climate problem. US per capita emissions are high, as are emissions in all rich countries, because from the way the contemporary world is structured, high living standards necessarily involve burning tons of fossil fuels. Greta Thunberg, after attracting incredible media attention for sailing across the Atlantic Ocean in a low-emissions way, thanked the people who helped her sail and then remarked that "we can't require from everyone to rely on people like this to sail you across an ocean, that is absurd."

In other words, we can't just ask people to give up the fruits of prosperity. Nor does it make sense to try to minimize the number of prosperous people. What the world needs, climatewise, is to develop and deploy technologies that will make prosperous lifestyles sustainable. If that can be done, the number of prosperous people is irrelevant.

The good news is that for electricity generation we have a number of zero-carbon technologies that work well. Hydropower generates cheap, clean electricity, and the only problem is that there aren't a number of promising new places to build dams. Nuclear power is more expensive, but it works fine and if you compare the risk and lethality of nuclear accidents to the number of air pollution deaths caused by properly functioning fossil fuel plants, it's clear that nuclear power is actually the safer option. Solar and wind power work well and are increasingly affordable. The problem is that the sun isn't always shining and the wind isn't always blowing. But short-term storage via batteries works well and is getting cheaper.

What doesn't yet work very well is "seasonal storage" where you could stockpile solar electricity during the long summer days and then use it during the short, dark winter months. But the total package of hydro plus nuclear plus renewables plus batteries really works. Taking climate change seriously means spending money to deploy it as rapidly as physically possible, even while continuing to research the seasonal storage issue in hopes of going all-renewable someday.

By the same token, electric automobile technology works great—it's just a bit pricey and at times the actual charging is inconvenient.

But that's a clear case of where taking the problem seriously and investing what it takes to build out a more robust charging network would encourage a much more rapid adoption of electric cars.

Transitioning away from internal combustion engines and fossil fuel electricity is basically a political problem—people don't like to have their lives disrupted, and entrenched interests don't want to lose money—but the technology works.

By contrast, there's no electric plane you can fly from New York to London. And there's no electric container ship that's going to move thousands of giant boxes across the Pacific. We can (and should) modernize building codes to allow the use of engineered wood in a wider range of circumstances, but as of yet it's impossible to conceive of a modern society without concrete and steel, and there is no commercially viable zero-carbon way of producing either.

These, along with a range of issues related to agriculture, are the difficult unsolved *technical* problems of climate change. They fundamentally require scientific progress, R&D funding, subsidies to deploy infant versions of potentially promising technology, and perhaps a bit of good luck. These are also the areas where American public policy could conceivably have the most leverage. Tweaking policy at the margin could induce Americans to fly a bit less, burn a bit less jet fuel, and emit a bit less $CO_2$. But doing everything in our power to encourage the invention of workable electric planes would have noticeable consequences for global emissions because if a plane like that worked, it would be broadly useful to everyone.

Obviously, this is all a gross simplification and there is an enormous amount that could be said about the details here. But it does capture the basic shape of the problem. We need to deploy the workable technologies we have much more rapidly, and we need to invest more in trying to solve the unsolved problems. And so the right climate question to ask about any policy that isn't directly related to energy is, Does it make it easier or harder to do those things?

It can't be denied that one billion Americans would mean higher emissions—largely because America is a rich country with high living standards—but it doesn't really make any of the fundamental problems we need to solve any harder. And the biggest logistical difficulty for growing the national population runs in tandem with the biggest logistical impediment to deploying the zero-carbon technology we already have—America has become a place that has a lot of difficulty building stuff, and we are going to need more stuff.

## We need to build more stuff

A bigger country will need a lot of new stuff. So will a zero-carbon economy.

At times and in critical ways it's largely the same new stuff. To accommodate more people, we need to knock down some existing houses and replace them with denser structures. To reduce greenhouse gas emissions, we need to knock down some existing houses and replace them with more modern and more energy efficient ones. Some of that is a question of money, but much of it is a question of the regulatory environment. Getting solar panels installed on my roof has involved battles with the Historic Preservation Review Board and visits to the Advisory Neighborhood Commission. Ultimately, the powers that be decided to let solar trump historic preservation. But when it came to installing energy efficient windows, preservation rules made me opt for a lower-performing more-expensive option rather than the windows I wanted. Most efficient of all, however, would be for some of the row houses on my block to be replaced by modern apartments, but obviously that's not in the cards.

But the same considerations also apply to civil engineering.

"Nearly every giant infrastructure project suffers from massive delays and cost overruns when they aren't shut down altogether," observes James Temple, the senior energy editor at *MIT Technology Review*, in a trenchant essay. "That all bodes terribly for our ability to grapple with the coming dangers of climate change, because it is fundamentally an infrastructure problem."*

There are as-yet-unsolved technical problems that need to be surmounted to build a zero-carbon economy. There are also plenty of workable technologies that simply need to be deployed much more rapidly. But the current setup of American politics and American life makes it difficult to conceive of a significant increase in the pace at which offshore wind and utility-scale solar projects are undertaken, much less massive new power transmission lines to move energy from the places where renewables are plentiful to the places where people live.

The climate change topic landed on the political agenda thanks to the work of the environmentalist movement. And certainly the steps needed to address it would have considerable environmental benefits, including most notably reductions in the massive public health harms associated with air pollution.

But on another level, infrastructure renewal on the necessary scale cuts against many of the neopastoralist sentiments associated with environmentalism. More prosaically, the same basic hyper-local planning paradigm that allows not-in-my-backyard (NIMBY) sentiments to triumph over new housing also hurts clean energy projects. "At best, Nimby pushback is raising costs through delays,"

---

*James Temple, "Climate Change Means the US Must Start Building Big Things Again," *MIT Technology Review*, January 15, 2020, www.technologyreview.com/2020/01/15/130892/climate-change-green-infrastructure-us-public-works-building-boom.

writes Mike Casey of wind power projects in the industry publication *Recharge*. "At worse, half-a-billion-dollar wind farms are dying because 50 people shouted at their county commissioners during a public meeting."[*]

Building a bigger America and building a cleaner America both require us to break out of the current dysfunctional veto-laden approach to building things, and find a way back to a future-oriented mind-set that says change is good.

And that means changes not just to the built environment, but to how we think about family life and the division of labor between parents and society writ large.

---

[*]Mike Casey, "US Wind Developers Are Losing the Online Battle Against NIMBY Groups," *Recharge News*, October 1, 2019, www.rechargenews.com/wind/us-wind-developers-are-losing -the-online-battle-against-nimby-groups/2-1-672133.

## CHAPTER 3

# The Dismal Economics of Child Rearing

B ack in 2017, the American fertility rate hit a record low of 1.76 expected births over the lifetime of the average woman. In 2018, it dropped to a brand-new record low of 1.72 births per woman.

Some of this reflects laudable trends, in particular an ongoing decline in the teen birth rate, more widespread availability of contraceptives—generally thanks to the Affordable Care Act—and more awareness of the benefits of superreliable forms of birth control like the IUD over more failure-prone methods like condoms or birth control pills that require adherence to a daily regime to work properly. Very high birth rates, meanwhile, generally reflect bad situations. Historically, women all over the world tended to have many children in large part because the child mortality rate was so high that giving birth to many children was the only reliable way to ensure that a few would survive into adulthood. Reliable contraceptives were not available, and women often lacked the legal, social, and cultural autonomy to control their own bodies.

These conditions continue to persist in significant parts of the world today and are a major tragedy. The big picture "demographic transition" is nothing to regret. Nor should we regret the more recent evolution of social norms in developed countries that have opened up more career opportunities to women and thus somewhat diminished the allure of motherhood.

But changing tastes actually *don't* explain the changes we've seen over the past forty years or so.

Back in 1972, American women told the General Social Survey that they would ideally like to have three children on average.[*] That's the first year for which data on this is available and may reflect a decline from an even higher ideal fertility earlier in the baby boom era. But the stated number fell pretty quickly over the next decade until 1980, when it was just a bit more than 2.5 children. That's the decline you'd expect to see driven by changing gender norms and women's rising career aspirations. Ever since 1980 there's been very little change in this indicator, and in the most recent survey it is only up to 2.6 children.[†]

Yet the actual number of babies being born keeps falling. As Lyman Stone from the Institute of Family Studies writes, "The gap

---

[*]General Social Survey, chldidel variable, https://gssdataexplorer.norc.org/variables/619/vshow.

[†]Julia Belluz, "The Historically Low US Birthrate Explained in 3 Charts," *Vox*, May 15, 2019, www.vox.com/science-and-health/2018/5/22/17376536/fertility-rate-united-states-births -women.

between the number of children that women say they want to have (2.7) and the number of children they will probably actually have (1.8) has risen to the highest level in 40 years.”*

One reason completed fertility ends up falling short of desired fertility is that men have a role to play in the process. But men's stated ideal number of children is only very slightly lower than women's—just about 0.04 children fewer on average—and the male-female gap on this metric has been consistent across the relevant time span. Another factor is that many couples end up having trouble conceiving and thus fall short of the number of kids they would ideally like to have. But infertility is not new, and because the state of medical science has improved over time, this pushes in the opposite direction.

What has changed is the economics. On the one hand, the cost of things you need to buy on behalf of kids (child care and education, mostly) keeps growing faster than the overall growth of national income. On the other hand, the structure of the economy keeps making it harder and harder for twentysomethings to achieve the kind of financial stability that prospective parents want. These dual forces both directly restrain the number of kids people have, and also tend to push people into starting families later in life, which often makes that second or third child harder to conceive.

There's nothing wrong, exactly, with consumption patterns changing over time as the economy changes. People these days go to the

---

*Lyman Stone, "American Women Are Having Fewer Children Than They'd Like," *New York Times*, February 13, 2018, www.nytimes.com/2018/02/13/upshot/american-fertility-is-falling-short-of-what-women-want.html.

movies less but watch television more than people did fifty years ago. As someone who happens to really like movies, I find this a bit regrettable yet obviously not a big deal in the grand scheme of things. But children are an important source of life satisfaction to many people in a way that moviegoing is not, so on the face of it, the fact that people are unable—and increasingly so—to have the number of kids they say they want to have is a legitimate source of social concern. The fact that having children in adequate numbers is also an important part of maintaining the ongoing project of American life only makes it more so.

## It's OK to talk about this

To conservatives, the idea that this is a valid cause for social concern tends to come obviously (though they then tend to shy away from the idea of doing anything about it).

Progressives, by contrast, tend to be quite open to a number of ideas that would help with the problem—child allowances, subsidized child care, student debt relief—but are somewhat strangely allergic to actually saying that it's a problem. That, in turn, tends to lead them to propose versions of those programs that are poorly structured, often featuring excessively narrow visions for what can or should be accomplished and creating strange financial incentives as people move up the economic ladder.

One reason for this "allergy" is a belief in some circles that talking about reproduction is per se racist. Marissa Brostoff, an editor at

*Jewish Currents*, for example, published a *Washington Post* op-ed arguing that "conservative lawmakers and right-wing vigilantes alike have adopted a seemingly new language for describing their antiabortion stance: the white nationalist discourse of the 'great replacement,' a conspiracy theory that holds that nonwhite immigrants are demographically 'replacing' whites throughout the West."*

She brought some solid evidence to the table for that thesis. But in the course of doing so she also swept the conservative writer J. D. Vance—who has an Indian American wife and a multiracial son—into the critique simply based on statements he had made in worrying about the American birth rate.

But if a white nationalist would be concerned with whether or not white children are being born, an *American* nationalist would worry about the fate of American families of all ethnic backgrounds. Indeed, the fertility decline in recent years has been concentrated in Black and Hispanic families rather than white ones. And programs to help families with children would, unless explicitly structured in racist ways, disproportionately help people of color. The median white American, after all, is forty-four years old, while the median Black American is thirty-four, and the median Hispanic American is just thirty. In other words, a much larger share of the white population is already out of the childbearing years and not in a position to take advantage of any new programs.

If we worry at all about racism in this regard, the worry should

---

*Marissa Brostoff, "How White Nationalists Aligned Themselves with the Antiabortion Movement," *Washington Post*, August 27, 2019.

probably be that America's large and electorally potent bloc of white senior citizens may be unwilling to do enough to support young families that they perceive as ethnically distinct. That reluctance to help out children who look different contributes to America's stingy welfare state,* and understanding the issue at least in part in nationalistic terms could be helpful in transcending ethnic divides and persuading people to take care of the entire national community.

The other line of discomfort comes from the feminist perspective.

Having fought for decades, if not centuries, to give women the right to control their reproductive destinies, feminists tend to be uncomfortable with the idea that people should be encouraged to have more children. On a personal level, women are also more likely to be beset by older relatives or well-meaning acquaintances badgering them about marriage and children and don't want to hear it from the government. Women also worry about the reality that they shoulder a disproportionate share of domestic labor burdens, and tend to suffer professional repercussions as a result.

These are totally reasonable concerns. It's also worth saying that there's nothing wrong with small families—my wife and I have one kid and that's plenty for us—and like everyone else, I know lots of people living happy and fulfilled child-free lives.

But America doesn't need some kind of coercive campaign to get people to have more children. It doesn't need to snatch people's birth

---

*Alberto Alesina, Edward Glaeser, and Bruce Sacerdote, "Why Doesn't the US Have a European-style Welfare State?" Brookings Panel on Economic Activity, September 7, 2001.

control. It doesn't need some kind of mass propaganda campaign to persuade people to have children. Preferences vary and that's fine. What we need to do is take seriously the claims to reproductive autonomy in both directions. People should be equipped with the tools they need to avoid pregnancy and childbirth, but also with the kinds of social supports that are needed to have and raise children. And that means recognizing that the natural evolution of the market economy really is making this approach harder and harder.

## Children and the cost disease

The key to understanding the problem is something called Baumol's cost disease, after William Baumol, who first described it. It's a very general economic principle, with important implications for the cost of child-related things.

His go-to example, however, was actually about music.

Along with fellow economist William Bowen, he observed that it takes the same number of musicians—four, by definition—to play a Beethoven string quartet today as it did when Beethoven first wrote it two hundred years ago. There has been no increase in the productivity of live classical music performances, and on some level there never will be. But Beethoven's Europe was a crushingly poor, low-productivity society compared with contemporary developed countries. Modern-day unskilled laborers live a life of incredible luxury—electric lights, plumbing, cell phones, television, HVAC, refrigerators—compared with the peasant farmers of the eighteenth century.

Skilled musicians, both in the past and today, earn a meaningful wage premium over unskilled laborers. Consequently, the same general increase in productivity that has driven up wages and living standards across the economy means that today's musicians earn much higher wages than the musicians of two centuries ago. But while workers in general are much more productive, our string quartets are not. Consequently, the cost of hiring live musicians to entertain at a party has absolutely skyrocketed even while the cost of keeping the room brightly lit or providing off-season fruit has plummeted.

Now, in the specific case of music this bad news is offset by the miraculous progress made in modern times in the field of recorded music.

Record players, the Walkman, the compact disc, the iPod, the smartphone, and now the modern digital streaming music service give any middle-class person who's even mildly interested in music access to a nearly unlimited library of tunes. Access to private live performances may have gotten worse, but overall access to music has improved enormously.

The basic problem of family economics is that taking care of small children is a lot like playing in a string quartet. Technological improvements have greatly improved our ability to take and share cute photos and videos of our kids but have only barely improved our ability to actually watch, take care of, and teach them. Running a day care center, a preschool, a summer camp, an afterschool dance class, or a weekend soccer league is inherently labor intensive. Technological change has made certain tasks related to communicating around the margins of these activities easier, but it hasn't allowed supervisors of children to meaningfully scale up their activities. That creates a basic cost-escalation dynamic that policy makers have not really addressed.

Everything else that gets talked about in this space is important too. It's true that the United States has been shamefully slow compared with some peer countries to provide subsidized child care. It's true that some jurisdictions have senselessly increased child-care costs with excessive or ill-considered regulation. And it's true that there are lots of good questions to be asked about how exactly elementary schools should be organized and curricula designed. But the cost disease lurks behind all of these topics. Productivity is slowly but surely growing throughout the economy, and wages are slowly but surely rising with it. That leaves labor-intensive sectors that don't benefit from rising productivity stuck with escalating costs that can't really be avoided.

## The opportunity cost of parenting

The cost disease refers in the first instance to the monetary cost of purchasing services. But the opportunity cost of doing things for yourself rises for the same reason.

This is important because, fundamentally, parenting is time-consuming even for families who have a child enrolled in school or other child-care arrangement. There are nights, mornings, and weekends. There are holidays and sick days. Summer vacations and postchildbirth recovery.

And while spending time with children is (mostly) a joy, there's also a lot of parenting-adjacent activity that's almost entirely a drag. There's extra laundry, packing lunches, scheduling appointments, filling out forms, scrubbing spills out of the carpet, and a million other logistical and support tasks. Over time there has been some productivity improvement in these fields—most notably the rise of washer/dryers and dishwashers—but very little of that has come in the most recent decades.

Because wages have gone up on average over this time period and continue to incrementally rise with each passing year, the opportunity cost of time spent on parenting has risen in line with the financial cost of child care. In practice, of course, most of this work is done by women, and women's wages have risen faster than men's over the past generation or two, making the opportunity cost increase especially large.

Most of these changes, to be clear, are good. Americans would not want to return to the material living standards of 1960 with rotary phones, three-channel televisions, inefficient cars, small houses, and no statins, beta-blockers, or SSRIs. But even change for the better requires adjustments. And we have not really adjusted our policies to consider the basic economics of modern family life. Indeed, to the extent that our policies have shifted, they've often shifted in the wrong direction—with higher education in particular becoming more burdensome at the worst possible time.

## The college cost shift

In 1910, fewer than 10 percent of American eighteen-year-olds finished high school, and only 18 percent of fifteen- to eighteen-year-olds were even enrolled in school. Across most of the country it was understood that the point of public schooling was to instill basic math and literacy skills and eight grades were sufficient to accomplish that. Secondary school, generally speaking, was a college preparatory curriculum for a narrow elite.[*]

Over the course of three decades that changed and by 1940 the median American youth had a high school diploma and more than 70 percent of appropriately aged teenagers were enrolled in high school.

That vast expansion was the fruit of the high school movement[†] that undertook to build and finance public high schools in communities all across the country. This was, naturally, a difficult undertaking, but it was also a logical and appropriate reaction to a growing realization that obtaining more schooling would pay off in the increasingly technologically sophisticated economy of the twentieth century.

Then came World War II, and in the immediate aftermath the United States appeared prepared to carry the logic of the high school

---

[*]Claudia Goldin, *The Race Between Education and Technology* (Cambridge, MA: Belknap Press, 2008), 195.

[†]See Claudia Goldin and Lawrence Katz, "Why the United States Led in Education: Lessons from Secondary School Expansion, 1910 to 1940," National Bureau of Economic Research working paper no. 6144, 2008, https://scholar.harvard.edu/lkatz/publications/why-united-states-led-education-lessons-secondary-school-expansion-1910-1940.

movement forward with a significant expansion of most states' public college and university systems. Between 1957 and 1965, for example, the University of California (UC) added six new campuses to the already extant UC, Berkeley, and UCLA along with eight new California State University campuses. These schools, and similar institutions in other states, were not quite free, but the fees to attend them were low and universally affordable on the basis of part-time or summer work.*

But backlash to the counterculture, the economic problems of the 1970s, and the conservative ideological climate of the 1980s and 1990s eventually pointed in another direction. While the high school movement held that because high school was valuable it should be provided as a service to the community, modern higher education policy reflects the view that because college is valuable, people should go into debt to purchase it as an investment. The government's role is to step in with subsidies to ensure that the debt is widely available and the interest rates are not too high.

This new paradigm has created all kinds of mischief—financing the launch of many low-quality for-profit ventures that no state legislature would ever deliberately appropriate funds for, encouraging a proliferation of questionable master's degree programs that serve as cash cows for universities, and often confusing low-income students into thinking they can't afford to go to college when in fact they can.

---

*Aaron Bady and Mike Konczal, "From Master Plan to No Plan: The Slow Death of Public Higher Education," *Dissent*, Fall 2012.

For our purposes, however, the most important consequence has been to create a kind of extended adolescence.

Most people aim to achieve a degree of financial stability and subjective respectability before starting a family. Once upon a time, that would have meant obtaining a farm of one's own or finishing up an apprenticeship. Later it might have meant finishing high school. Today, for actual and aspiring members of the broad professional class, it typically means college. Pushing back the potential window for the commencement of family formation tends to risk, for biological reasons, the ability of people to have as many kids as they'd have liked. This is probably an unavoidable aspect of modern life. But the switch to debt-financing of education has served to further delay the arrival of financial stability by saddling college grads with debt service payments that weigh heavily during what would otherwise be the primary years for family formation.

College is still clearly "worth it" despite the high costs. As a team of researchers at the Federal Reserve Bank of St. Louis concluded after a 2019 study of the evidence, "College and postgrad degree holders generally earn significantly higher incomes than non-grads." They did, however, find that "the conventional wisdom about college is not as true as it used to be" in part because of the rising cost.[*] Over the long run, a lifetime of higher earnings outweighs the burden of a few years of heavy debt accumulation. The problem from the

---

*William Emmons, Ana Hernández Kent, and Lowell Ricketts, "Is College Still Worth It? It's Complicated," St. Louis Federal Reserve, February 7, 2019, www.stlouisfed.org/on-the -economy/2019/february/is-college-still-worth-it-complicated.

standpoint of family life is that this "long run" arrives much later in life than the traditional time for people to get married, buy homes, and have kids.

Meanwhile, a separate set of economic pressures has started to weigh mightily against family formation for America's working-class majority.

## The safety net's marriage penalties

It's no secret that the past generation or two of economic growth in the United States has been very unequally shared. Incomes at the top have soared, while those in the middle have risen much more slowly.*

What's a little less widely appreciated is the mixed role of public policy in generating these trends. On the one hand, inspired by ideas from the political right, policy makers adopted a broad suite of legal and regulatory changes that tended to increase incomes at the top. On the other hand, a series of Democratic Party administrations have succeeded at expanding the social safety net and making the federal income tax code somewhat more progressive.

According to Congressional Budget Office data, means-tested safety net programs have boosted incomes for the bottom 20 percent

---

*My favorite source for this data is Chad Stone, Danilo Trisi, Arloc Sherman, and Jennifer Beltrán, "A Guide to Statistics on Historical Trends in Income Inequality," Center on Budget and Policy Priorities, updated January 13, 2019, www.cbpp.org/research/poverty-and -inequality/a-guide-to-statistics-on-historical-trends-in-income-inequality.

of the population by 65 percent in 2016 along with a more modest boost for the next 40 percent.*

This in turn means that the details of safety net design have become increasingly important influences on the course of American life. Upward of 40 percent of American households with children receive means-tested benefits from the Supplemental Nutrition Assistance Program (SNAP), Medicaid, or Supplemental Security Income, and that trend is only going to continue if, as seems likely, more states eventually accept federal funds to further expand Medicaid.

One relevant fact is that these programs are generally designed to include large "marriage penalties" in which the income gained by adding a second adult to a household tends to rapidly crowd out benefits. This is often discussed, to the extent that it is discussed at all, in terms of its impact on couples' decisions about whether or not to get married at the time of the birth of a child. A 2016 study by the American Enterprise Institute and the Institute for Family Studies, for example, found that couples with a baby under two years old and an income between about $24,000 to $79,000 a year "are about two to four percentage points less likely to be married if they face a marriage penalty in Medicaid eligibility or food stamps."†

The real impacts, however, are larger. Not only do marriage penalties discourage parents from getting married, the lack of a married

---

*Congressional Budget Office, "The Distribution of Household Income, 2016," July 9, 2019, www.cbo.gov/publication/55413.

†W. Bradford Wilcox, Joseph Price, and Angela Rachidi, "Marriage, Penalized: Does Social-Welfare Policy Affect Family Formation," Institute for Family Studies and American Enterprise Institute, July 2016.

partner discourages people from having children. And these issues intersect.

Some of the most striking marriage penalties afflicting working-class households occur through the tax code these days. A single mother earning $20,000 a year will receive a fairly generous $3,367 earned income tax credit (EITC). But if she marries the baby's father and then a couple of years later they have a second kid and a $40,000 household income, their EITC drops to $2,628. They'd also lose Medicaid benefits in most states. The $700 marriage penalty in the EITC may not sound like a huge amount, but every dollar counts for lower-income families. And these benefits are simply not very generous in the first place. A married couple with two kids earning $50,000 who has a third baby gets an extra $728 in EITC benefits—not enough to cover a year's worth of diapers and wipes.*

The basic shape of things is that while the safety net has ensured that family income in the bottom 40 percent of the distribution has continued to grow, it's not well structured to help people achieve stable family life—joining with the basic Baumol effect to discourage people from actually having as many children as they'd like. And to address the issues facing families all up and down the economic spectrum would require the country to think in more expansive terms about what social assistance is for and how generous we should be with it.

---

*See the Center on Budget and Policy Priorities' handy calculator featured in "Policy Basics: The Earned Income Tax Credit," www.cbpp.org/research/federal-tax/policy-basics-the-earned-income-tax-credit.

# PART II

# The
# Solution

## CHAPTER 4

# Taking Families Seriously

The way to improve typical American families' lives and enhance the nation's long-term prospects for national greatness is both complicated and simple: start taking family formation seriously as a priority, and start treating the costs of raising children as a major consideration in the design of social policy.

A number of Bush-era federal "marriage promotion" initiatives turned out to be largely hot air.* But ridding the social safety net of disincentives to marry, though fiscally somewhat costly, would be an excellent idea.

Then beyond that, we, as a society, ought to put some real resources behind the common sentiments that children are our future

---

*Katherine Boo, "The Marriage Cure," *New Yorker*, October 18, 2003, www.newyorker.com /magazine/2003/08/18/the-marriage-cure.

and parents have the hardest job of all. That means committing to paying for kids' medical care, to providing schooling and child-care options that are grounded in a realistic understanding of modern schedules, and to building wider social norms that support the idea that what parents do is important.

And while there's much more to life than money, it starts with acknowledging that kids simultaneously cost money and make it harder to work long hours, so families with kids need extra financial support.

## The Family Fun Pack

The current debate in the United States is so far off the mark in terms of really living up to society's obligation to parents that the most serious plan for dealing with it comes not from any of Washington's many mainstream think tanks, but from the People's Policy Project— essentially a one-man show run by Matt Bruenig, an eccentric socialist who along with his wife, *New York Times* columnist Elizabeth Bruenig, is a parent of two young kids.

They whimsically call their proposal the Family Fun Pack, and while it's rigorous in its details, it's also strikingly simple in concept. What if we, as a society, took all the things that we broadly agree all young families need and actually gave them to all of them?[*] The

---

*Matt Bruenig, "The Family Fun Pack Makes Parenting Easy for Everyone," People's Policy Project, February 15, 2019, www.peoplespolicyproject.org/2019/02/15/the-family-fun-pack-makes-parenting-easy-for-everyone.

implications of this basic thought turn out to be fairly dramatic, featuring universal health care for all children, paid parental leave for all parents, a "baby box" program for newborns, and a comprehensive system of childcare and preschool programs.

Health-care policy could consume an entire book of its own. But setting that aside, we're left here with an ambitious but sensible policy agenda.

The "baby box" refers to an idea that was pioneered by the government of Finland way back in the 1930s. Helena Lee of the BBC profiled the Finnish baby box about seven years ago and described it as "a starter kit of clothes, sheets and toys that can even be used as a bed." It is, literally, a cardboard box that "contains bodysuits, a sleeping bag, outdoor gear, bathing products for the baby, as well as nappies, bedding and a small mattress."* In 2017, the government of Scotland hopped on the baby box bandwagon.†

While doing so, Scottish first minister Nicola Sturgeon explained that the box isn't just practical assistance to new families, it's "a powerful symbol of our belief that all children should start life on a level playing field."‡

This is, of course, also something that most Americans say we believe in. And English-language press coverage of the Finnish baby boxes has sparked enough enthusiasm that Finnbin and other commercial

---

*Helena Lee, "Why Finnish Babies Sleep in Cardboard Boxes," BBC News, June 4, 2013, www .bbc.com/news/magazine-22751415.

†Kelly Richman-Abdou, "Finland Gives Every Parent-to-Be a Baby Box Kit Full of Essentials," *My Modern Met*, December 3, 2018, https://mymodernmet.com/finnish-baby-box.

‡Cammie Finch, "Scotland Plans to Give All Expecting Mothers Generous Boxes of Baby Supplies," *My Modern Met*, October 19, 2016, https://mymodernmet.com/baby-box-scotland.

providers of similar products have emerged with the popular baby shower gifts. They're genuinely useful and make great gifts (my wife and I were given one before our son was born and we loved it), but they're essentially a yuppie affectation and thus accomplishing roughly the opposite of the social meaning Sturgeon outlined.

Compared with the other aspects of the fun pack, the baby box is both very cheap and also not that important as a matter of substance. But the symbolism is worth dwelling on because it captures the overall spirit of a better way to think about family policy. The box aims to be of high quality, providing things that are good enough that affluent families want to use them—things that are appealing enough that imitation boxes are sold for profit in the United States. We should give the boxes to everyone who has a baby—they're not welfare boxes for needy families, they're the basic equipment for all children.

That, of course, "wastes money" in the sense that most of the families who get a box could afford to buy one (or equivalent products) out of pocket. But universal provision ensures that middle-class and affluent families with real political voice are invested in maintaining high standards, which ends up helping the relatively disempowered poor. And universal provision also emphasizes a correct desire to subsidize children and child rearing as such—a socially valuable activity that deserves to be encouraged just as we use taxes to discourage things like smoking and excessive alcohol consumption.

The logistics and cost of extending these same principles into areas beyond the box are more difficult. But the principles are sound and we should follow them where they lead.

# A universal child allowance

A shocking fact about the United States of America is that 21.1 percent of our children are living in poverty, compared with 11.3 percent of German children and just 9.3 percent of Swedish children even though the United States is richer on average than either Germany or Sweden.*

This is because, fundamentally, a market economy does not magically allocate extra wages to people who have children even though children are expensive. European welfare states address this problem by providing extra money to parents of young children. The exact amount of money varies from place to place—the Netherlands is on the stingy side and Belgium is very generous—but there's a universal recognition that assistance is needed.

Americans are, of course, aware that children cost money. But our main policy remedy for this, the child tax credit, is severely inadequate. For starters, at $2,000 per child per year it's stingier than Germany's *Kindergeld* benefit, which starts at €2,448 per year for the first child and becomes slightly more generous for subsequent children.† But the credit also phases in and phases out in a complicated

---

*These are figures for poverty among children age 0–17 using the Organization of Economic Cooperation and Development's (OECD) relative poverty metric. The US government defines children as including 18-year-olds and calculates poverty two different ways, both of which are different from the OECD's way. But it still adds up to a disproportionate share of children living below the poverty line. OECD, "Poverty Rate," https://data.oecd.org/inequality/poverty-rate.htm.

†Rachel Stern, "Kindergeld: What you need to know about Germany's child support payments," *The Local*, July 12, 2019, www.thelocal.de/20190712/everything-you-need-to-know-about-receiving-kindergeld-in-germany.

way on the theory that affluent families don't need the financial help and very poor families essentially aren't working enough to deserve the help.

Both of these notions are deeply entrenched aspects of the American political psyche, but they come at some real cost.

Nobody needs to cry for people earning $300,000 a year and not getting their child tax credit. But the failure to provide the child benefit to families who "don't need it" does reflect a failure to take supporting children seriously as a broad social obligation. Rich people are, after all, allowed to go to the park or take books out from the library or drive on the interstate on the same terms as everyone else even though they don't really "need" access to those public services. The point is that when we think a service is important, we provide it on equal terms for all. You adjust for the fact that rich people have more money by charging them higher taxes. Precisely because the federal government has a progressive tax structure, the right way to think about providing child benefits to affluent families is that it involves childless rich people paying a cross subsidy to affluent families with two or three children. That's not the most pressing social obligation in the world by any means, but it's a perfectly reasonable idea and a good statement of values that raising families is an important form of participating in society.

The low-end version of this is considerably more urgent, because the consequence of refusing to give benefits to the neediest families is that millions of children are subject to intense material deprivation despite living in one of the richest societies in all of human history.

The theory that refusing to give cash benefits to parents with scant labor market earnings will inspire them to get full-time jobs is interesting. But we now have an ample historical track record that shows definitively that this is not the case. It's based, among other things, on a completely unrealistic view of how unemployment dynamics in the broader economy work as well as of the complicated barriers to full-time work that people living on the margins of society often face. It's completely correct to posit that, ideally, we should be offering people in need a hand up in terms of mental health care and substance abuse treatment, job training, transportation support, and other things they'd need to sustain employment. But this is a difficult-to-execute vision, and there's no reason to wait years or decades to figure it out when we could start cutting child benefit checks to the neediest families tomorrow.

Most congressional Democrats have come together around a legislative proposal they call the American Family Act (AFA) that would greatly ameliorate the situation. Their plan is to deliver a child benefit worth $300 a month for all kids aged five and under plus $250 per month for kids aged six to sixteen. This would be administered as a monthly check rather than a year-end rebate so that parents can meet their kids' needs as they arise, rather than needing to plan around a once-a-year windfall. Nobody would be too poor to claim the benefit, though it would begin to phase out for single parents earning more than $130,000 and married couples earning more than $180,000.

---

*Sykes et al., "Dignity and Dreams: What the Earned Income Tax Credit (EITC) Means to Low-Income Families," *American Sociological Review*, October 10, 2014, https://journals.sage pub.com/doi/abs/10.1177/0003122414551552.

Democrats structured this plan primarily to try to be a cost-effective antipoverty program, and it would lift about 4 million children out of poverty and cut the deep poverty rate for kids by nearly half.[*]

They don't talk about this as a fertility program. But Lyman Stone, the conservative researcher whose work on the fertility gap we discussed earlier, calculates that its implementation "could also boost fertility, adding tens or hundreds of thousands of births each year," closing a quarter of the fertility gap all on its own.[†] What's more, a relatively small technical adjustment could increase its punch even further. Research from Australia's experiment with a "baby bonus" payment to new parents suggests that people are more sensitive to up-front payments—new babies, after all, come with a bunch of new expenses right away and typically have an initial negative impact on parents' earnings—than to long-term payouts.

The current structure of the American Family Act is to pay $50 more per month in a child's first six years of life than in the remaining years. If you tweaked that instead to be a flat $250/month child allowance with a $3,600 initial bonus, you'd do even more to spark family formation and more to help parents at their moment of greatest need.

Relative to the AFA approach the up-front bonus would do less on paper to push people over the poverty line because poverty is measured in terms of annual income. But it's the same amount of

*Dylan Matthews, "Democrats have united around a plan to dramatically cut child poverty," *Vox*, May 2, 2019.

†Lyman Stone, "Cash for Kids? Assessing the American Family Act," Institute for Family Studies, March 12, 2019.

money. And delivering it faster at the maximum point of need would leave low-income families better off rather than worse off. Making the bonus genuinely universal by including all families, meanwhile, would make the program more expensive. But transferring income from affluent childless households to *all* families with children regardless of income status is conceptually sound and would make a child bonus/child allowance policy more sustainable in the long run. Indeed, true universalism is probably the best bet for addressing the main political obstacle to thinking clearly about family policy.

## Programs for the poor

When the subject is old age, the American government delivers two big programs—Social Security and Medicare—which are designed to offer a universal guarantee of a decent and reasonably dignified retirement.

But when the subject is children, with the important exception of K-12 schools, things look very different. America is stuck with a conservative movement that wants to be stingy with overall spending on social assistance and then a liberal movement that wants to target scarce resources at those with the greatest need. The American welfare state recognizes that more children equals higher needs, and thus delivers more help to a low-income single mother of three than to a single mother of one. But the married couple earning $50,000 with two kids isn't going to be pushed below the poverty line by a third, so they get very little. A professional couple earning

$130,000 with one kid isn't going to be anywhere near objective material deprivation if they have a second, so they don't get any help at all.

Left-wing politicians have begun to tout the idea of free college for all qualifying students. But this idea remains intensely controversial even among left-of-center people.

Sandy Baum, an economist at the Urban Institute who specializes in the higher education needs of disadvantaged students, writes that "a national free-tuition plan would provide disproportionate benefits to the relatively affluent while leaving many low- and moderate-income students struggling" and thus "exacerbate inequality even as they promise to level the playing field."*

Her math and that of other skeptics of the free college concept can be nitpicked, but it's fundamentally difficult to dispute. If your only concern is the tilt of the playing field, a narrowly targeted program is a good way to level it.

That's why virtually all Democratic plans for "universal" childcare provision are structured as income-linked subsidies. The goal is to provide assistance in proportion to objective household need, meaning that poor families get a lot of help but more comfortable ones get very little. In effect, these sorts of programs take family structure as a fixed factor—they "penalize" marriage because married couples are more financially secure and less in need of help, and they do little to help median-income and higher-income families

---

*Sandy Baum and Sarah Turner, "'Free tuition' is the opposite of progressive policymaking," *Washington Post*, May 3, 2019, www.washingtonpost.com/outlook/free-tuition-is-the-opposite-of-progressive-policymaking/2019/05/03/4767edc8-6c1b-11e9-a66d-a82d3f3d96d5_story.html.

shoulder the cost of raising children because those costs won't push those families into penury.

Under the circumstances, it's worth considering what America might look like if over the past four generations we'd constructed public schools as sliding-scale subsidy programs that aim to target the neediest families. Clearly, many families who are currently enjoying free public education could afford to curtail some of their other consumption and pay tuition instead. But over the longer term, drastically increasing the financial costs to middle-class families would result in smaller middle-class families. The guarantee of free public education wasn't designed as an explicitly "natalist" policy, but its universal design reflects a sense that children are on some level a communal obligation and not just a consumption choice made by parents.

Applying that same kind of standard across the board would cost a lot of money, which is one important reason that we haven't done it. The existence of the public school system, by the same token, isn't cheap. But it's important.

And over the long haul, universal programs probably do more to help the neediest than microtargeted ones do anyway. The old saying about this is that "programs for the poor become poor programs"—programs that are easily subject to political attack—while universal programs garner stronger support. The political science on this is not entirely unambiguous, but there is enough evidence on it to suggest that there ultimately isn't a real trade-off between helping the poor and helping everyone. The political fight to establish a universal program does involve larger dollar signs, but it can be an easier fight to win because it includes more people in the winner's circle.

But going universal also lets you tap in to arguments that people of more conservative inclinations may find more compelling. Libertarian economics won't support the culturally conservative goals of strong families and national greatness. But a robust welfare state can—if we design it appropriately.

## Parental leave

The conversation around family policy in the United States is probably most advanced on the topic of paid parental leave. America is currently an enormous global outlier in its decision to provide new parents with zero weeks of guaranteed paid leave.

Elsewhere in the developed world, practice varies quite a bit from place to place, but the absolute floor is about three months of leave with at least partial pay, with Germany, Japan, and Sweden offering more than a year in some cases.

Reasonable people can disagree about the best way to strike the balance here. Longer leave times are a nice benefit for some parents (though in my experience it's also not unheard of for new parents whose employers offer generous leave to be quietly glad when it's over so they can spend more time in the company of adults), but it's also costly. What's more, whatever the formal legalities, very long leave times are necessarily going to be disruptive to careers.

By the same token, there are a number of interesting value-laden questions about how to split the leave across two partners and how to treat single parents equitably. Sweden, famously, has an interesting system that allocates bonus extra leave time specifically to fathers to encourage men to play a larger role in child rearing. That's very appealing to some people with egalitarian ideas about gender, though in other respects it seems wasteful and even arguably unfair to mothers.

What's not open to reasonable dispute is that zero weeks of paid leave is not the right number of weeks.

There's really no better example of America's accepting the hegemonic logic of free markets over every other conceivable value than this current system. Providing some leave rather than no leave would, obviously, impose some costs on businesses and on nonparents. But the United States is not an impoverished society teetering on the brink of mere subsistence. Nobody thinks that it's actually a good idea for brand-new parents to have to return to work immediately—basic medical recovery from childbirth generally takes several weeks on top of the parenting aspects—and, obviously, in some sense the cost to society for *someone* to look after the newborn has to be incurred one way or the other.

If we believe at all in the idea that having and raising children is a valuable activity, then mandating some kind of decent minimum of paid leave is literally the least we could do.

## Preschool for all

Nobody thinks it would be appropriate or workable to mandate anything close to five years of paid parental leave, and yet in most jurisdictions public school doesn't start until kindergarten. Before that, families are on their own.

The historical origins of this are easy enough to understand. School was conceived of as primarily about teaching kids to read, so it wasn't provided to children who were too young realistically to be doing that. More recently, inspired by the finding that low-income students tend to start kindergarten already behind their higher-income peers, there has been a lot of interest in the potential benefits of earlier schooling. Many cities and even a few states now have pre-school programs for four-year-olds, and there's considerable interest in progressive circles in further expansions.

This has generated a substantial literature on the question of whether publicly funded preschool programs are effective at improving underprivileged kids' lives or at closing various gaps in educational attainment. Some of the studies have very optimistic findings. Jens Ludwig and Douglas Miller, for example, took advantage of the fact that Head Start initially launched in America's three hundred poorest counties to compare outcomes for kids in those counties with kids in counties that just barely missed the cutoff. They found positive impacts on child mortality, high school graduation rates, and college attendance.[*] Diane Whitmore Schanzenbach and Lauren Bauer compared outcomes for kids who attended Head Start programs to their siblings who did not and found long-term effects

---

[*]Jens Ludwig and Douglas L. Miller, "Does Head Start Improve Children's Life Chances: Evidence from a Regression Discontinuity Design," *Quarterly Journal of Economics*, February 2007.

on graduation rates, college attendance, and even self-control, self-esteem, and improved parenting practices in adulthood.[*]

On the other hand, a study by Mark W. Lipsey, Dale C. Farran, and Kelley Durkin, which looked at a Tennessee preschool program that admitted families by lottery, found that positive effects faded out by the second or third grade.[†]

These results are not strictly contradictory, because they were from different studies across different time ranges. What's more, while randomization studies like the one from Tennessee provide the highest quality of evidence, they are also relatively rare and sometimes have relatively low statistical power compared with broader methodologies like the ones used on the Head Start studies. But more important, the obsessive focus on whether or not preschool provides big long-term benefits to children ignores the obvious short-term benefits to parents of giving them a safe, well-run, socially sanctioned place for their children to go during the day.

Once the government is in the business of providing preschool, it should try to make the programs as educationally enriching and effective as possible. But the case for doing it isn't just that it can make kids smarter, it can also make it much more viable for people to have children in the first place. And that, in turn, is a big reason to favor

---

*Diane Whitmore Schanzenbach and Lauren Bauer, "The Long-Term Impact of the Head Start Program," Brookings Institution, August 19, 2016, www.brookings.edu/research/the-long-term-impact-of-the-head-start-program.

†Mark W. Lipsey, Dale C. Farran, and Kelley Durkin, "Effects of the Tennessee Prekindergarten Program on children's achievement and behavior through third grade," *Early Childhood Research Quarterly* 45, www.sciencedirect.com/science/article/pii/S0885200618300279.

efforts to create genuinely universal preschool programs that—just like K-12 public schools—offer spots to all families rather than targeted subsidies for the poor.

## Universal day care

For even younger children we tend to talk about day care rather than preschool, though of course the conceptual boundaries here are somewhat fluid.

But while some school districts have incorporated preschool programs into their public school systems, nobody seems willing to contemplate a truly universal system for younger kids.

Even a very left-wing Democrat like Elizabeth Warren, who ran for president on a plan to provide free medical care to the whole country, conceived of her day-care program in means-tested terms. Her program would, in essence, cap child-care costs at 7 percent of household income—a huge boon to lower-income families but a much smaller assist to more affluent ones.*

This may simply be the limit of what's considered politically realistic. But these plans, by design, continue to leave child-care costs as a huge burden on middle-class families. A 2018 poll for *The New York Times* asked people who have or expected to have fewer children than they considered ideal why they hadn't had more kids. The number

---

*Sarah Kliff, "Elizabeth Warren's universal child care plan, explained," *Vox*, February 22, 2019, www.vox.com/policy-and-politics/2019/2/22/18234606/warren-child-care-universal-2020.

one answer was that child care is too expensive. Number three was worries about the economy. Number four was "can't afford more children," and number five was that the parents had waited to start having kids until they achieved financial security and then ran out of time.[*] (Number two was wanting more time with existing children.)

Addressing these interlocking cost concerns in a narrow way for the lowest-income families is fine, but it's clear that the systematic cost of raising children is a huge influence on American society further up the income spectrum. We could, in theory, save even more money by deciding to charge tuition for K-12 schools with an exemption for the poorest families. However, that would increase cost burdens on the middle class and further reduce fertility rates below what women say they want.

But we should be seizing the opportunity to do the opposite and take every reasonable step possible to make responsible child rearing broadly affordable. That's a great way to promote basic human flourishing and to nurture and sustain the long-term future of the country.

## Summertime blues

Much as children who are too young to read still need a safe and enriching place to spend the day, there's something fundamentally

---

*Claire Cain Miller, "Americans Are Having Fewer Babies. They Told Us Why," *New York Times*, July 5, 2018, www.nytimes.com/2018/07/05/upshot/americans-are-having-fewer-babies -they-told-us-why.html.

odd about the way America's public school system vanishes during the summer months.

While it's true that summer vacation is, in its way, a cherished ritual of youth, it's also true that public schools are important public services that provide critical functions for children and families. It wouldn't make sense to have a city's fire or police department close up shop for months at a time just because wearing the uniforms in the summer heat is uncomfortable.

To the extent that this oddity has figured in the policy conversation, the main topic of interest has been what's known as summer learning loss—the idea that kids actually regress in their academic competencies over the summer months. The classic study on this, done way back in 1996, found that summer vacation corresponds to a decline in achievement roughly equivalent to one month of in-school time. The decline was bigger for math than for reading because kids at all points of the income spectrum experienced math decline, whereas reading loss was seen only in low-income students.[*]

Some more recent research has called those findings into question.

Paul von Hippel writes that he "used to be a big believer in summer learning loss," but "my colleagues and I tried to replicate some of the classic results in the summer learning literature—and failed."[†]

Hippel's doubts, however, turn out to most relate to the idea that

---

[*]Harris Cooper, Barbara Nye, Kelly Charlton, James Lindsay, and Scott Greathouse, "The effects of summer vacation on achievement test scores: A narrative and meta-analytic review," *Review of Educational Research* 66, no. 3, 227–68, http://journals.sagepub.com/doi/10.3102/00346543066003227.

[†]Paul von Hippel, "Is Summer Learning Loss Real," *Education Next*, Fall 2019.

summer learning loss is uniquely hard on low-income students. His own preferred source of data on the subject, from the Measures of Academic Progress tests, shows pretty clearly that keeping kids out of school for long stretches of time impedes their progress—he simply thinks that it impacts kids across class lines about equally.

Given how contentious most proposed reforms of the K-12 school system are, the idea of providing academic programming during the summer months looks like something that would pretty clearly work. Having children in classrooms practicing their reading and math is going to lead to better reading and math outcomes than not doing it—the logic is obvious, and the data is unambiguous.

But beyond the academic considerations, the extended school closures of spring 2020 are a reminder that the absence of school is an incredible inconvenience to parents over and above its educational purpose. Modern children are not providing economically useful labor on farms during the summer months. And in most cases they don't have full-time stay-at-home parents to take care of them either. Kids are, instead, enrolled in a rotating series of camps and child-care arrangements that parents need to pay for out of pocket. The quality of these programs is uneven enough that the finding that we don't see a uniquely harmful impact on students in low-income schools is a genuinely surprising finding in its own right. But given the explanation that students in low-poverty schools experience exactly the same learning loss, the moral seems to be that existing summer programming is either uniformly bad or else it's extremely difficult for even the best programs to compensate for a lack of alignment with ordinary school curricula.

If the status quo were year-round schooling, it seems extremely unlikely that anyone would be agitating for an extended summer shutdown. The financial and logistical pain for parents would be too much to bear over and beyond the plain risk to academic achievement. What's more, especially in high-poverty communities, the school is often a center of broader service provision—giving kids access to free meals, a library of books, rudimentary medical screenings, and other services that shouldn't just vanish during the summer.

Switching to year-round schooling from the status quo would be easier said than done. Many school buildings are not equipped with appropriate climate control for the hot summer months. You couldn't just ask teachers and other school staff to significantly extend their annual working hours without also offering them higher salaries— to say nothing of dealing with the myriad collective bargaining agreements that would need to be changed. And because the whole existing teacher workforce is composed of people who deliberately bought in to teachers' unusual work schedules and have built lives around them, even that trade-off wouldn't necessarily be straightforward.

Because American schools are administered in a very decentralized way, there's no real prospect for a uniform national change anyway. The best path forward is probably to take advantage of that reality to experiment a little.

It would be interesting to see at least a few jurisdictions (perhaps ones where the physical infrastructure is already suitable for year-round operation) try true year-round schooling with higher teacher salaries. If this does turn out to generate appreciable improvements in academic outcomes, it would make a lot of sense to put in the work to expand that model.

Alternatively it's at least possible that the academic results here would prove disappointing. It would be nice to see other jurisdictions experiment with concurrent models like town-run summer camps where kids would engage in traditional American childhood summer activities, except organized by the public sector and available free to the entire community; alternatively, a more market-oriented approach with "summer enrichment vouchers" could also be worth trying. There's a whole range of plausible ways to meet families' practical need to have a place for young children to go during summer days, and we should try them all.

What's really *not* plausible is the idea that it's sustainable to subject families to the ever-growing cost of caring for and educating children. Ignoring the mismatch between the school year and the work year has been the status quo for so long that we take it for granted.

## Days off

Many of these same basic considerations apply during the school year.

My son's school, like public schools across America, closes for holidays like Veterans Day and the day after Thanksgiving. Because I live in Washington, DC, where an unusually large share of people work for the federal government, a healthy slice of the city's public school parents do have the day off. But even in DC most people don't get these days off (I don't), and throughout the rest of the country this kind of mismatch between school holiday schedules and private employers is endemic.

Even above and beyond the official holidays, our school calendar is also littered with "professional development" and other closures.

With regard to early education and summertime, I've made the case that the public should pay what it takes to provide comprehensive services. In terms of days off and holidays, it probably makes more sense to move in the other direction and try to make private employers behave more like the public school system. The downside to reducing the number of workdays in the private sector is that it would risk making the country somewhat poorer on average. But the United States is already the richest large country on the planet, and our citizens enjoy the biggest houses, largest cars, and best household appliances of any nation.

But Americans also work extremely long hours, putting less time in on the job than you see in poor countries but more than in any of the other thirty richest nations on earth.[*]

One reason for this is that while in European countries it's standard to have three, four, five, or even six weeks of paid vacation as a government guarantee, in the United States the minimum number of paid vacation days is zero. Of course parents and nonparents alike would enjoy some extra time off. But given the practical demands of

---

*Dora Mekouar, "Why Americans Work More Than Their Foreign Peers," *Voice of America*, September 7, 2018, https://blogs.voanews.com/all-about-america/2018/09/07/why-americans -work-more-than-their-foreign-peers.

caring for children, additional time spent outside the paid labor market is an inherently pro-family step.

Beyond the merits of additional vacation time, there may be a strong argument for specifically creating more—and more robust—national holidays to ensure that a larger share of the population actually gets our existing federal holidays off.

Evidence for this comes from research that the sociologists Cristobal Young from Stanford and Chaeyoon Lim from the University of Wisconsin published back in 2014. They have shown that subjective emotional well-being rises by 5 percent on average during the weekend. That's easy enough to understand—everyone enjoys a day away from the grind. But the really interesting thing they found was that unemployed people are happier on the weekend too.

Young and Lim find that "workers and the unemployed experience remarkably similar increases in emotional well-being on weekends and have similar declines in well-being when the workweek begins," and this is "in large part because social time increases sharply on weekends for both workers and the unemployed."[*]

The basic idea here is that if weekends were fun just because you didn't have to work, they wouldn't be fun for unemployed people. But what makes the weekend enjoyable is that it's an opportunity to socialize with friends and family, thanks to everyone collectively not working. Which is to say that widespread observance of Veterans Day as a day off would probably generate more happiness than

---

*Cristobal Young and Chaeyoon Lim, "Time as a Network Good: Evidence from Unemployment and the Standard Workweek," *Sociological Science*, February 18, 2014, www.sociological science.com/time-network-good.

giving everyone a spare vacation day to use whenever they want to—even though superficially more flexible time off should be better.

An ideal policy mix is probably some combination of the two—both a minimum floor of flexible vacation days for everyone and a law mandating overtime pay rates for people who work on recognized federal holidays, thus encouraging employers to think twice about asking people to work on what are supposed to be days off. Under any conceivable policy framework, of course, plenty of people—from cops and nurses to air traffic controllers and bus drivers—are going to need to work on holidays, and the very fact that so many people have the day off provides an incentive for stores and movie theaters and restaurants to stay open and make money serving them. Flexible vacation days are an indispensable tool for people whose jobs involve unusual schedules, and giving a decent guaranteed floor of them along with more holidays should be a no-brainer.

But fundamentally the case of holiday and vacation time is the exception that tests the general principle. If we want to have a family-friendly society, then we need to provide, at public expense, safe and reasonably enriching places for children to be during normal working times. Compressing the number of hours the typical person works per year is part of the solution to that problem. But there's no way the normal work schedule is going to shrink to the current public school schedule. We fundamentally need to expand the amount of child-centered programming, acknowledge that it will cost money, and accept it as a price worth paying.

That's an adjustment of budgetary priorities but it is also, more broadly, what we as a society deem important.

# A family-friendly culture

The structure of family life is, fundamentally, at least as much a question of norms and culture as it is of material conditions.

But as Daniel Patrick Moynihan famously said, "The central conservative truth is that it is culture, not politics, that determines the success of a society. The central liberal truth is that politics can change a culture and save it from itself."

I've focused primarily on policy change because that's the main lever we have. The hope, however, is that policy change spurs larger changes. Changing the design of the social safety net to ensure that working-class people don't lose benefits if they get married should have a modest impact on marriage rates. But a higher marriage rate should have its own secondary impact, in which more couples see married peers in their social groups and neighborhoods, which changes their own thinking. Similarly, if providing more and better benefits to parents and families leads more women, at the margin, to have their first child somewhat earlier, that also shifts expectations for their peers.

We're not going to suddenly return to the norms of an earlier era, nor would that necessarily be desirable. But some reconsideration of what's really important in life could be useful.

Derek Thompson, an economics correspondent with *The Atlantic*, has observed that across significant swaths of America a new quasi religion he calls workism has taken root. The key tenet of this faith is that a job should be not just a job, but also a source of enduring meaning in one's life. But as he observes, "The problem with this gospel—Your dream job is out there, so never stop hustling—is that it's a blueprint for spiritual and physical exhaustion."[*] Americans spend more hours per year on the job than any comparably rich country, and those long hours are at best pointless and at worst destructive. Erin Reid, a professor now at McMaster University in Canada, did a study of workers at a global consulting firm where long hours are the norm. She found that while fathers who explicitly asked to work shorter hours to spend more time with their family were penalized, managers actually couldn't detect any deterioration in job performance from dads who just pretended to work more than they actually did.[†]

By contrast, as Sarah Green Carmichael has written for *Harvard Business Review*, there is compelling evidence across multiple lines of research that "overwork and the resulting stress can lead to all sorts of health problems, including impaired sleep, depression, heavy drinking, diabetes, impaired memory, and heart disease."[‡]

Now, to an extent there's nothing wrong with people wanting to find work that they enjoy. Indeed, as humanity moves ever further away from bare subsistence and toward prosperity, it's entirely reasonable for people to make job choices that emphasize factors other

---

[*]Derek Thompson, "Workism is Making Americans Miserable," *The Atlantic*, February 24, 2019, www.theatlantic.com/ideas/archive/2019/02/religion-workism-making-americans-miserable/583441.

[†]Erin Reid, "Why Some Men Pretend to Work 80-Hour Weeks," *Harvard Business Review*, April 28, 2015, https://hbr.org/2015/04/why-some-men-pretend-to-work-80-hour-weeks.

[‡]Sarah Green Carmichael, "The Research Is Clear: Long Hours Backfire for People and for Companies," *Harvard Business Review*, August 19, 2015, https://hbr.org/2015/08/the-research-is-clear-long-hours-backfire-for-people-and-for-companies.

than the pursuit of money. But the idea of work as an ultimate source of meaning tends to set people up for failure and frustration over and above the practical problems of overwork. One of the nice things about emphasizing relationships with family, friends, and community as a source of meaning is that this is an attainable goal for virtually everyone.

Work-as-meaning, by contrast, is both something of a privileged niche (essentially available only to those who have a "career" rather than a mere "job") and is limited even for the advantaged. Economic life, fundamentally, is competitive. Even someone lucky enough to make a living doing something truly enjoyable is always going to be faced with the prospect of someone else who is more successful at the same thing, or someone younger who is threatening to close the gap. More emphasis on relationships with our kids, our friends, our nieces and nephews, or the children in our neighborhoods is something that's much more accessible and egalitarian. And while Congress can't pass a law mandating that people reorient their thinking in this way, such a reorientation would naturally be both part of the case for stepping up investment in family life and a consequence of doing so.

Norms and material conditions, meanwhile, are likely to move in the same direction. Raising children is easier if other people you know are also doing it. A town or a neighborhood with many children in it is more likely to have family-oriented activities, restaurants with crayons for the kids, an inclination to invest in building playgrounds, and a deep market of experienced babysitters available for hire.

Last but by no means least, while part of building a supportive culture for families should include doing more to support parents, another part of it should be trying to do less to shame and stress them. A remarkable amount of advice is doled out by the media, the government, and quasi official organizations with little regard for the difficulty of complying or the often poor quality of the evidence.

## Chilling out

The tendency toward excessive shaming begins immediately after birth because contemporary society is in the grips of a modest moral panic about breastfeeding. Breastfeeding is, obviously, a viable and appropriate means of feeding an infant. It's an experience some mothers find rewarding or pleasurable, and under the right circumstances it can have a lower direct financial cost than buying formula.

But for many mothers it's stressful, painful, inconvenient, or otherwise difficult and only becomes more so as they attempt to rejoin adult society or even temporarily leave the newborn in the care of others. For them, formula may be a convenient alternative that is easily worth the money. Huge swaths of the medical, media, and political establishment, however, have become deeply invested in a "breast is best" narrative that's based on extremely low-quality correlational evidence. The data is very clear that kids who are weaned later have better outcomes on a range of indicators. But the data is also clear that these kids have mothers who are richer and better educated. Kids who ride home from the hospital in luxury cars end up doing better in school and earning more money than those who ride home in pre-owned cars, but everyone understands (I hope) that buying a Mercedes won't make your children smarter.

To properly study the impact of something like breastfeeding, you need either sophisticated statistical controls or else randomized data. When economist Emily Oster went looking for high-quality evidence on breastfeeding for her book *Cribsheet*, she found that "it seems reasonable to conclude that breastfeeding lowers infant eczema and gastrointestinal infections" and also that there may be "a small reduction in ear infections in breastfed children."[*]

That's not nothing, and it certainly suggests that all else being equal you should breastfeed rather than switch to formula. But we are talking about relatively minor—and, critically, exclusively short-term—impacts here and nothing that people should be subjecting themselves to extraordinary levels of pain or inconvenience over.

Much the same is true of the endless wrangling over "screen time" for young kids, an area where, again, most of the studies finding a correlation between watching lots of television and below-average outcomes are failing to control for unequal household income and educational attainment. As Oster also observes, messages on this subject from the American Academy of Pediatrics (AAP) and others don't seriously consider what the alternative is. "The AAP guidelines imply that this alternative activity is something more enriching:

_____

*Emily Oster, *Cribsheet* (New York: Penguin Press, 2019), 77.

reading books with dad, running on the track, discussing current events with grandma, etc."* And, obviously, yes—spending all day watching television is not optimal child development.

But real life is about trade-offs. If letting a kid watch some television lets you cook a meal, put a sibling to bed, hold down a job, or otherwise conduct the necessities of life, then why not? There's no sense in working middle-class parents into such a state of anxiety about their parenting or shaming lower-income families for being unable to fully ape the lifestyle choices of more affluent ones.

It might also be useful to remind parents of some good news. Today's children are *dramatically* safer than today's adults were when we were kids, with death rates for young children having fallen by more than half since I was born in 1981 and for teens by nearly that much.

Last—and relatedly—we should consider relaxing in some key ways in terms of our public policy measures. Present-day child care in the United States is paradoxically unaffordable for parents but also unremunerative for the workforce. And a big part of the reason is regulations, which have tended to get stricter for no particularly clear reason. Regulators have tended to reduce the maximum ratio of children to caregivers, which raises costs sharply. Taking advantage of the fact that practices in this regard vary from state to state, Diana Thomas of Creighton University finds that "an increase in the child-staff ratio requirement for infants by one infant is

---

*Emily Oster, "Screen Time for Kids Is Probably Fine," *FiveThirtyEight*, June 18, 2015, https://fivethirtyeight.com/features/screen-time-for-kids-is-probably-fine.

associated with a decrease in the cost of child care of between 9 and 20 percent."[*]

Given that dramatic change in cost structure, it's striking that there's no clear evidence that lowering the ratio improves outcomes for kids at all.

Current trends, unfortunately, tend to point in the opposite direction. Starting just as my son aged out of day care, Washington, DC, where I live, was putting in place new regulations requiring day care workers to have at least associate degrees. A *Washington Post* report on the initiative optimistically said the new rules "put the District at the forefront of a national effort to improve the quality of care and education for the youngest learners."[†]

I hope that turns out to be true. But the initiative is not grounded in any clear evidence that restricting the early childhood workforce in this way will actually make things better, while it fairly obviously will raise costs and push families either out of the city, out of the formal child care system, or into having fewer kids. Meeting children's actual needs is hard enough for both families and the public sector. The last thing we need to do is make it even harder than it needs to be.

And that includes not going overboard in describing our environmental problems.

---

[*]Diana Thomas, "Regulation and the Cost of Child Care," Mercatus Center working paper, August 17, 2015, www.mercatus.org/publications/regulation/regulation-and-cost-child-care.

[†]Michael Alison Chandler, "D.C. among first in nation to require child-care workers to get college degrees," *Washington Post*, March 31, 2017, www.washingtonpost.com/local/social-issues/district-among-the-first-in-nation-to-require-child-care-workers-to-get-college-degrees/2017/03/30/d7d59e18-0fe9-11e7-9d5a-a83e627dc120_story.html.

## Climate and kids

Speaking with Ta-Nehisi Coates at a Martin Luther King Jr. Day event in New York in January 2019, Alexandria Ocasio-Cortez explained her generation's embrace of left-wing politics, "Millennials and Gen Z and all these folks that come after us are looking up, and we're like, 'The world is going to end in 12 years if we don't address climate change, and your biggest issue is how are we gonna pay for it?'"*

This is of course not true in any literal sense, and after a couple of days of controversy AOC was induced to walk it back.

But even though everyone knows the world will still be around into the 2040s and beyond, rhetoric along these lines has become a fairly common activist gloss that attempts to raise the urgency with which world leaders address the topic. As someone who would really like to see world leaders address climate change with more urgency, I don't like to spend my time nitpicking activist rhetoric or second-guessing their tactics. But the fact that there is not, in fact, a looming tipping point toward apocalypse is relevant to the main subject of this book, so we do need to get a bit nitpicky.

David Wallace-Wells, for example, wrote a book called *The Uninhabitable Earth: Life After Warming*, which explores the worst-case scenario and is explicitly part of a project designed to make

---

*William Cummings, "'The world is going to end in 12 years if we don't address climate change,' Ocasio-Cortez says," *USA Today*, January 22, 2019.

people more alarmed.* A project that, in my experience, has in fact succeeded in making lots of progressives very anxious about the impact of climate change on them and their children. But Wallace-Wells himself has written more recently that based on the latest estimates from the International Energy Agency and "given only current carbon policies, which nearly everyone studying climate considers terribly weak, the world is on track for about 3 degrees Celsius of warming by 2100, which could, if existing pledges were implemented, be brought down as low as 2.7 degrees."

Thanks to President Trump, Brazilian president Jair Bolsonaro, and others, the world has actually gotten *further* from meeting the official internationally agreed target of limiting the world to 1.5 degrees Celsius of warming. But that's matched by the good news that worst-case scenarios now look less likely than ever largely because the economic case for coal has gotten worse, and for solar it has gotten better, regardless of what policies are adopted. As Wallace-Wells writes, "What was recently the best to hope for now seems vanishingly unlikely, and what was the worst to fear much less likely, too."†

Now to be clear about this, 2 or 3 degrees of global warming is still extremely bad. We are talking about upward of 150 million extra deaths from air pollution, massive increases in storm damage and coastal flooding, huge refugee flows, and mass population displacement.

---

*David Wallace-Wells, "Time to Panic," *New York Times*, February 16, 2019, www.nytimes.com/2019/02/16/opinion/sunday/fear-panic-climate-change-warming.html.

†David Wallace-Wells, "We're Getting a Clearer Picture of the Climate Future—and It's Not as Bad as It Once Looked," *New York*, December 20, 2019, http://nymag.com/intelligencer/2019/12/climate-change-worst-case-scenario-now-looks-unrealistic.html.

The idea of doing almost nothing to avert this catastrophe and then congratulating ourselves because it wasn't literal human extinction is borderline obscene.

But the distinction is relevant to some key issues. World War II, for example, was obviously a catastrophic human tragedy, leaving upward of 70 million people—most of them Allied civilians—dead. Business as usual regarding climate change risks a cataclysm on that scale, inflated up to account for the fact that the world's population has quadrupled since 1940.

That's not human extinction, but it is extremely bad and quibbling about exactly how to characterize the disaster can feel cheap. But the distinction does matter.

In the Avengers movies, for example, Thanos wants to kill half the world's population to avoid natural resource depletion. Philosophers would debate the ethics of this plan, but it would basically make sense if the downside of ecological unsustainability was actual human extinction. But killing billions to save hundreds of millions is just bad math and doesn't require any complicated philosophical arguments at all.

By the same token, the implicit population ethics of the common argument that not having children is a good way to reduce your carbon footprint don't really make sense. Large families don't generate more emissions because children are particularly resource intensive (quite the opposite, they are smaller than adults and don't drive cars), it's because they contain more people. You could just as easily reduce emissions by encouraging people to commit suicide. And even though the COVID-19 pandemic caused a drastic reduction in short-term greenhouse gas emissions by shutting down the economy and a longer-term change in the trend by killing people, nobody is glad it happened. If the risk were that one additional person would tip the whole world onto a path of inevitable extinction, that would be different. But limiting the actual problem with climate change limits the possibilities for human flourishing. That's a huge problem and it's worth doing a lot to avoid, but you don't need to cut off the flourishing itself.

What is more, the fastest and cheapest way to increase the national population is also one of the best ways to help the world adjust to warming—let people move.

# CHAPTER 5

# More and Better Immigrants

Policies aimed at growing the national economy through having more kids work with a built-in time lag. Preschools and day care centers will not magically materialize the day after a law authorizing their construction is passed. And even if the checks for something like a new child allowance program can begin to flow immediately, any children who result will take twenty to twenty-five years to become adults who fully participate in the national economy. And there will be five to ten additional years on top of that before they genuinely enter their prime working years.

Immigrants, by contrast, arrive at our shores good to go from day one.

Already today in America, nannies, hotel cleaners, forklift operators, fruit pickers, table bussers, roofers, NBA stars, computer programmers, and everything in between* arrive as adults and get to work essentially right away. Without them, America would already have fallen behind China in the big economic aggregates, and most of us would live poorer, harder, less interesting lives as individuals.

Immigration and immigrants have, however, become *the* hot-button political issues of our time. Originally that hot-button debate focused on the unfortunate legacy of some poor policy choices made in the late 1980s and mid-1990s that created a settled block of millions of people living and working in the United States illegally. Efforts to find a sensible and humane resolution to that problem appeared close to bearing fruit in 2007 and then even closer in 2013, but that work was scuttled primarily by demagogues trading on fear for personal and political gain.†

In subsequent years, the demagogues' voices have grown only louder and more powerful with racist conspiracy theories about "white genocide"‡ and "the great replacement"§ bubbling closer to the surface of conservative politics.

---

*According to a Brookings Institution analysis of Current Population Survey (CPS) data, the top industries employing immigrants are (in order): private households, accommodations, warehouses, management and administration, agriculture, food service, construction, high-tech manufacturing, and information technology. See Audrey Singer, "Immigrant Workers in the US Labor Force," Brookings Institution, March 15, 2012, www.brookings.edu/research /immigrant-workers-in-the-u-s-labor-force.

†For an in-depth portrait of the legislative negotiations that almost bore fruit, see Ryan Lizza, "Getting to Maybe," *New Yorker*, June 17, 2013, www.newyorker.com/magazine/2013/06/24 /getting-to-maybe.

‡Jane Coaston, "The Scary Ideology Behind Trump's Immigration Instincts," *Vox*, November 6, 2018, www.vox.com/2018/1/18/16897358/racism-donald-trump-immigration.

§Sarah Wildman, "'You will not replace us': A French philosopher explains the Charlottesville chant," *Vox*, August 15, 2017, www.vox.com/world/2017/8/15/16141456/renaud-camus-the-great -replacement-you-will-not-replace-us-charlottesville-white.

Alongside this increasingly paranoid rhetoric has come a grow-ing hostility to a broader range of foreign-born people. The problem, according to Trump-era conservatives, turns out to be *not* just ille-gal immigrants. Refugee resettlement levels have been repeatedly cut.* The idea that Central American asylum seekers constitute an "invasion" of the United States has featured in rhetoric from the president of the United States to the El Paso Shooter and everyone in between.† Trump is making it harder for the spouses of high-tech guest workers to work legally in the United States,‡ and has made it harder to get student visas and harder for foreign-born recent col-lege graduates to get permission to work in the United States.§

He's also proposed legislation that would slash the total volume of *legal* immigration to the United States by 50 percent.

The high-level conservative contentions that entry to the United States should be controlled by law and that permission to live here should be dictated more by national interest and less by happen-stance make perfect sense. But the proposal to make immigration more "merit based" while simultaneously halving the overall level

---

*Dara Lind, "Trump slashed refugee levels this year. For 2019, he's slashing them even further," *Vox*, September 18, 2018, www.vox.com/2018/9/17/17871874/refugee-news-record-history -asylum.

†Alexia Fernandez Campbell, "Trump described an imaginary 'invasion' at the border 2 dozen times in the past year," *Vox*, August 7, 2019, www.vox.com/identities/2019/8/7/20756775/el -paso-shooting-trump-hispanic-invasion.

‡Monica Nickelsburg, "Trump administration starts cracking down on H-1B visa approvals and work permits for spouses," *GeekWire*, February 25, 2019.

§Nadine El-Bawab, "Trump's tough student and work visa policies are pushing legal immi-grants to Canada," CNBC, February 26, 2019, www.cnbc.com/2019/02/25/trumps-student -and-work-visa-policies-push-legal-immigrants-to-canada.html.

reveals a dangerously backward view of the situation.* The thinking seems to be that immigration is, at best, a kind of necessary evil, so the goal of reforming immigration policy should be to cut immigration as much as possible while minimizing the economic fallout.

This is fundamentally backward and, like the rest of the contemporary right's approach, reflects a cramped and paranoid view of foreigners. Great American leaders knew otherwise.

"America is open to receive not only the opulent & respectable Stranger, but the oppressed & persecuted of all Nations & Religions," George Washington told newly arrived Irishmen in 1783. He assured them they'd be "wellcome [sic] to a participation of all our rights & previleges [sic], if by decency and propriety of conduct they appear to merit the enjoyment."

But, critically, Washington's vision wasn't primarily about charity or helping others. It was about building the kind of country he wanted the United States to become. Greatness would require great people. America would need more than it had.

The contemporary debate around immigration is often framed around an axis of selfishness versus generosity, with Donald Trump talking about the need to put "America first" while opponents tell heartbreaking stories of deportations and communities torn apart. A debate about how to enforce the existing law tends to supersede discussion of what the law ought to say.

All of this misses the core point. Immigration to the United

---

*Tara Golshan, "Trump endorsed an immigration bill that probably won't pass. It still matters" *Vox*, August 3, 2017.

States has not, historically, been an act of kindness toward strangers. It's been a strategy for national growth and national greatness.

Few of our problems can be solved by curtailing immigration. Many could be solved by welcoming more foreigners to our shores. Trying to get better at choosing immigrants is a perfectly reasonable idea. But as things stand, on balance immigrants would be good for the country if we got even better at selecting them, and we'd want *more* immigrants rather than fewer.

## Ruthless pragmatism on immigration

The three fundamental facts of immigration policy are as follows:

* The country needs more people, and immigration is an easy way to get more people.
* Immigration is beneficial to native-born Americans and extremely beneficial to immigrants, and in general we should be more welcoming.
* A very large and politically influential share of the population is much more skeptical of immigration than it should be.

America desperately needs responsible public figures who can navigate the tensions between the second and third points in order to address the first one.

On one hand, it is a shame to see prominent people talking down any broad class of immigrants or giving succor to demagogues' fears. On the other hand, there is no sense in pro-immigration forces in American politics wedding themselves to outlier unpopular positions or pushing obviously unviable open borders schemes and then allowing the demagogues to win all the elections and govern the country.

What's needed, in practice, is a relentlessly pragmatic approach to expanding immigration and that means trying out some ideas and seeing what sticks.

A hypothetical community renewal visa concept I will discuss in Chapter 6 seems potentially promising in this regard. So does the idea of special visas for health-care professionals, which I'll describe in more detail later in this chapter. Streamlining the student visa process, so that any student with the ability to get in to a selective school and with the means to pay full tuition can easily do so, seems like a no-brainer. As does inviting the foreign-born graduates of selective American colleges and graduate schools to stick around and work. Given the extent to which cultural (or to be blunt, racial) fears seem to drive much of immigration politics, it might be interesting to explore the idea of fairly free and open immigration from Canada, Australia, the Anglophone Caribbean, America's NATO allies, or some other subset of countries that seems popular.

Several years ago I was involved with hiring a well-regarded Canadian-born journalist who, at the time, was residing in London. Never having really given it much thought before, I was taken aback by how difficult it was to get a visa for her. After all, in all the furious intensity of the immigration policy debate, nobody ever seems to be worrying that twentysomething Canadian journalists are going to come pouring across the border to mooch off our substandard health-care system and act polite to everyone.

Under the current paradigm, activists and members of Congress fear that more immigration of *any* kind will automatically mean squeezing out immigrants from Latin America. But it doesn't need to work that way. If there are groups of people it would be sensible to let in, an effort should be made to build political support for granting them permission. After all, on the merits different kinds of immigrants are complementary to one another. If we have more highly educated professionals moving here, then we will also have more demand for cooks and roofers and nannies and all the rest. The key point is that immigration is much more beneficial than many people realize.

## The Mariel boatlift

Some of the most important evidence for the benefits of immigration stems from a 1980 incident known as the Mariel boatlift, which today is probably best known to people who aren't labor economics nerds from the Al Pacino movie *Scarface*.

The Cuban economy was facing a sharp downtown, and roughly ten thousand Cubans attempted to apply for asylum in Peru by occupying the grounds of the Peruvian embassy in Havana. It was a moment of crisis for the Castro regime, which it tried to wriggle out of by pulling a little jiujitsu on its enemies in the United States. For decades

America had a policy of extraordinary generosity to people fleeing communist Cuba—far more generous than our approach to would-be immigrants from other parts of Latin America in a way that was maintained by foreign policy priorities and ethnic politics in Florida.

But on the Cuban side, just as the East German government erected a wall to prevent its citizens from fleeing to the West, the Castro government tried to make it hard for Cubans to flee to the United States.

Tried, that is, until April 1980, when it announced that Cubans were free to leave. In particular, the port of Mariel was opened to anyone who wanted to flee the country—provided someone was willing to pick them up. Cuban Americans, inspired by ethnic solidarity and anti-Castro zeal, answered the call and began piloting boats to take Cubans to freedom in America. Across a span of fewer than six months, 125,000 Cubans arrived in the United States, until the US and Cuban governments acted jointly to shut down the boatlift pipeline.

Contemporary reports that the boatlift was deliberately filled with people released from Cuban prisons and mental hospitals were greatly overstated. Nonetheless, this was pretty close to the reverse of a well-organized and "merit-based" immigration system. Castro's goal was to release a pressure valve on domestic discontent and also embarrass the United States by deliberately overwhelming Florida's practical capacity or political willingness to absorb Cuban refugees. And it worked. The influx of refugees created major logistical problems in South Florida and proved to be a serious political headache for Jimmy Carter.

But precisely because the boatlift was such a wild and crazy turn of events, it's a fascinating period to study to understand the impact of immigration from Latin America. And not coincidentally, it's been the subject of a high-profile scholarly duel for decades.

Something to note, though, is that while both journalistic and academic treatment of the issue tend to focus on the *conflicts* between scholars—because that's what's interesting—for policy-making purposes we should also pay attention to the areas in which they actually agree, because that goes to show how far removed the area of reasonable disagreement between dispassionate observers is from fears gripping a large swath of the population.

The first blow in the battle was leveled by David Card, a University of California, Berkeley, economist who is himself an immigrant from Canada.

Card is something of an iconoclast who was a pioneer in driving the economics profession's empirical turn—an approach that's fairly dominant today but that was novel in the late 1980s and early 1990s, when he was making a name for himself. The idea is that economists should try to use statistical tools to understand how the economy really works rather than insist that simple supply and demand charts tell you everything you need to know. He's probably best known today for pioneering work on minimum wage increases, work that found no adverse impact on unemployment and that served as inspiration for a later set of researchers and advocates on this topic.[*]

---

[*]See Card's book with Alan Krueger, *Myth and Measurement: The New Economics of the Minimum Wage* (Princeton, NJ: Princeton University Press, 1995).

Card later recounted that this work "cost me a lot of friends" and that many people in the field "thought that in publishing our work we were being traitors to the cause of economics as a whole."*

Card similarly tackled a supply and demand question in his 1990 paper "The Impact of the Mariel Boatlift on the Miami Labor Market."

What he found was that the impact was, in one sense, profound. The size of the labor force in the Miami metropolitan area increased by 7 or 8 percent within six months. By contrast, the total US working age population has increased by only about 4 percent over the past ten years. And the impact on the low-skill workforce in Miami was even more dramatic than that. Fifty-six percent of the Marielitos had no high school education and a further 9 percent hadn't completed the twelfth grade.

Cuba, in other words, wasn't sending its best people. And the results, according to immigration pessimists, should have been dismal.

And in some respects they were. The murder rate in Miami surged temporarily as city services seemed overwhelmed by the newcomers. A three-day riot in some of Miami's Black neighborhoods partially inspired by perceived labor market competition with the newcomers left thirteen people dead. But in wage and salary terms, Card found, basically nothing happened: "The Mariel influx appears to have had virtually no effect on the wages or unemployment rates of less-skilled workers, even among Cubans who had immigrated earlier."

---

*Douglas Clement, "Interview with David Card," *The Region*, December 2006, www.minneapolis fed.org/publications/the-region/interview-with-david-card.

Whites, Blacks, non-Cuban Hispanics, and Hispanics all saw no ill effects on the labor market outcomes.

Card doesn't like political arguments and has no public position on either minimum wage increases or immigration levels. But the implications of his study for policy are pretty clear—if even an enormous and completely chaotic influx of unskilled foreigners can be so benign for natives, then natives have nothing to fear from any realistic immigration policy, a person could actually propose.

But in life nothing is so simple.

Enter George Borjas. Himself, like Card, an immigrant—from Cuba no less—and also a well-regarded empirical labor economist, ensconced at Harvard's Kennedy School of Government. But while Card shies away from political fights, Borjas relishes them, memorably dismissing donors to the immigration-friendly Center for Global Development as "open borders plutocrats" and casting himself and his immigration-skeptical worldview colleagues as the true champions of American workers. Similarly, while Card tends to skip somewhat casually from one topic to another and disengage after publishing a few papers, Borjas is all in on research documenting the downsides of immigration. He even has a paper showing that the collapse of the Soviet Union, by sending many talented Soviet mathematicians to the United States, hurt American mathematicians' ability to publish in top journals.[*]

Borjas would, naturally, look askance at Card's putative finding

---

[*]George J. Borjas and Kirk B. Doran, "The Collapse of the Soviet Union and the Productivity of American Mathematicians," National Bureau of Economic Research working paper no. 17800, February 2012, https://www.nber.org/papers/w17800.

that even a Mariel-scale influx of immigrants did no harm to anyone's wages.

So in 2017, he published a reanalysis of the Miami data in the *Industrial and Labor Relations Review* charging Card's study with essentially asking the wrong question.* Borjas observes that while the overall increase in the size of the Miami labor market was large, the increase in the supply of workers who had not finished high school was positively enormous—a 20 percent increase.

"The unbalanced nature of this supply shock suggests that we should look at what happened to the wage of high school dropouts in Miami before and after Mariel," he writes. "By focusing on this very specific skill group, we obtain an entirely new perspective of how the Miami labor market responded to an exogenous supply shock."

The news is not good, with Borjas crunching the Current Population Survey numbers to estimate a wage drop for native-born workers of 10 to 30 percent. Even in its initial draft form, first circulated in 2015, these findings were a sensation written up by immigrant-skeptical pundits in *The Atlantic* and *National Review*, aired respectfully in *The New Yorker*, and cited by former attorney general Jeff Sessions at his confirmation hearings.† White House senior adviser Stephen Miller cited it from the White House briefing room as his

---

*George Borjas, "The Wage Impact of the Marielitos: A Reappraisal," *Industrial and Labor Relations Review*, October 2017.

†David Frum, "The Great Immigration-Data Debate," *The Atlantic*, January 19, 2016; Mark Krikorian, "The Facts on Immigration," *National Review*, November 7, 2016; Kelefa Sanneh, "Untangling the Immigration Debate," *New Yorker*, October 24, 2016; Senate Judiciary Committee Hearing, January 10, 2017.

main exhibit to justify the Trump administration's efforts to reduce legal immigration.*

But there's also been ferocious pushback to Borjas.

Michael Clemens, a senior fellow at the Center for Global Development, whose work includes trying to persuade countries to more aggressively pursue openness to immigration as a global economic development strategy, pointed out that Borjas was slicing the data *extremely* thinly. In response to the concern that Card's sample of working-class Miami residents did not adequately match the characteristics of the Marielitos, Borjas examined specifically the labor market outcomes of non-Hispanic men without high school degrees between the ages of twenty-five and fifty-nine ("prime-age" workers in labor market economist jargon).

This does create a statistical sample whose wages ended up falling below the pre-boatlift trend—but it's a sample that includes just seventeen individuals.

By contrast, looking at a broader universe of high school dropouts shows wages simply continuing on trend, and looking at all Miami workers who didn't go to college shows an increase.

At the same time, Giovanni Peri, a UC, Davis, economist who is sort of the anti-Borjas, churned out paper after paper underscoring the benefits of immigration and coauthored a study with Vasil Yasenov that essentially replicates Card's initial work except that it uses more modern statistical methods. They found the same thing Card

---

*Jerry Iannelli, "White House uses debunked Mariel Boatlift study to propose immigration crackdown," *Miami New Times*, August 3, 2017.

found but also confirmed Borjas's finding that if you look exclusively at the seventeen prime-age non-Hispanic men without high school diplomas in the sample, their wages went down.

No other subgroup has this feature and Borjas's sample is extremely small, so Peri, Yasenov, and Clemens characterize it as a statistical artifact that arises essentially from arbitrarily cherry-picking data.

That pretty swiftly degenerated into some fairly nasty academic name-calling with Borjas's critics accusing him of malfeasance and Borjas accusing them of being paid shills of the plutocracy. The whole thing is a fascinating story, but the really important thing to take away from it is not the disagreement but how narrow the disagreement actually is.

## Immigration is really good

After all, there are just not that many high school dropouts in America.

According to the census, 90 percent of American adults have a high school diploma or equivalent, and Hispanics and the elderly are usually unlikely to have finished high school. Consequently, the prime-age non-Hispanic dropout population is not just small in the Miami survey data, it is a small and idiosyncratic group of people writ large. The argument is whether a cataclysmically huge influx of poorly selected immigrants was harmful to the labor market prospects of a small minority. There's no disagreement in this academic duel that *most* Miamians were fine.

Nobody would or should propose that the United States routinely increase the size of its labor force by 7 percent over a six-month period. At that rate, the US population would double in five and a half years, and in twenty-five years the country would hold 9 billion people. But there's no reason to believe that people even vaguely approaching that number want to move here. To the extent that you want to take away from Borjas's research that a Mariel-scale influx of uneducated workers would be a bad idea, then by all means do so. But I think a better takeaway would be that even an enormous and almost comically poorly designed influx of migrants worked out just fine for the typical Miami native, even according to the leading immigration-skeptical researcher.

Indeed, careful examination tends to suggest that there are important easy-to-overlook *benefits* to the migration of even the least-skilled workers.

Consider seasonal agricultural labor, one area in which it's pretty clear that the whole point of immigration is to recruit workers who won't demand higher pay.

An excellent 2017 study by Michael Clemens along with Hannah Postel and Ethan Lewis looked at what happened in the mid-1960s when the United States ended the Bracero program that allowed farmers to import Mexican guest workers to do farm labor.* By comparing wage trend states that had lots of Bracero workers to those that had few Braceros and those that had none whatsoever, they

---

*Michael A. Clemens, Hannah M. Postel, and Ethan G. Lewis, "Immigration Restrictions as Active Labor Market Policy: Evidence from the Mexican Bracero Exclusion," IZA Discussion Paper Series, January 2017.

show that kicking out the guest workers had no impact on pay for farmworkers.

That doesn't mean the laws of supply and demand were magically repealed. It means that landowners changed their strategy. For some crops, like tomatoes and sugar beets, producers were able to switch to more mechanical harvesting techniques—compromising on quality in the case of tomatoes.

For other crops—including asparagus, strawberries, lettuce, celery, and cucumbers, for example—mechanization techniques were not available, and production simply fell. Wages did not rise; instead, Americans learned to live with reduced produce variety. It's striking that even the Trump administration has come to recognize the broad social value of seasonal agricultural workers, responding to the coronavirus crisis by streamlining the visa process out of fear that shutting down American consulates in Mexico would make it impossible to recruit enough workers.

The same impact on variety exists on the retail and service side of the economy as well. If you visit a place with few immigrants from Mexico—France or Fargo or what have you—you don't find that taqueria workers are earning vastly more money than their counterparts in Texas. You find that there are few good places to buy tacos. This isn't the end of the world, any more than an asparagus shortage would be an acute social crisis, but that's exactly why eliminating foreign-born workers doesn't boost wages. People simply make do without the variety that immigrants provide.

More broadly, a somewhat tired debate exists between people who argue that immigrants are needed to "do the jobs Americans won't do" and those who counter that for an appropriate wage you can always find someone to do a job.

What this dichotomy misses is that there are many jobs that simply won't be done under circumstances of constrained supply and high wages. And this will have secondary impacts down the line. A study by Patricia Cortés and José Tessada, for example, finds that when more low-skilled immigrants enter a metro area, you end up with college-educated professional women working more hours and earning more money because they can rely on the help of more housekeepers and babysitters.* Increasing the supply of unskilled workers, in other words, can also increase the supply of skilled workers.

None of which is to deny that there is a case for more selectivity. But the basic framework in which we approach selectivity should be positive and optimistic. Even very unskilled workers can, in appropriate contexts, contribute significantly to the living standards of native-born Americans. What we ought to be doing is acting more deliberately to ensure that immigration is being used as a powerful tool to address serious problems rather than allowing it to be driven largely by happenstance. But the basic evidence on happenstance-driven immigration is genuinely quite positive, and with a more selective framework the case for significantly increasing the overall volume of immigration would be overwhelming.

---

*Patricia Cortés and José Tessada, "Low-Skilled Immigration and the Labor Supply of Highly Skilled Women," *American Economic Journal*, July 2011.

## The ridiculous RAISE Act

That, of course, is not how the contemporary anti-immigration right sees things. They have instead rallied around the RAISE Act (Reforming American Immigration for Strong Employment) originally authored by Senators Tom Cotton and David Perdue and later embraced by President Trump as exemplifying his vision of what he terms a "merit-based" immigration system.

The way it works is that the current main categories of visas would be overhauled in favor of a new system that would allocate green cards based on how many "points" can be amassed in a scoring system.

More points are earned for things like speaking English, having a high-paying job, and having solid educational credentials. The basic idea, which is by no means crazy, is to try to select immigrants who are likely to do well in the American labor market, earning a good living and contributing significantly to the tax base and the economy. The scoring system also sensibly considers your age, noting that a would-be immigrant who is far from retirement age is likely to contribute a lot to the Social Security and Medicare Trust Funds and thus be a worthier candidate than a similarly situated older person. Last but by no means least, they acknowledge that there are other considerations that might plausibly factor in to the "merit" calculus, including an ability to win Olympic medals or secure a Nobel Prize.

But while both the idea of a focus on points and the broad contours of the scoring make some sense, the particulars are borderline absurd.

The overall scheme is, allegedly, patterned on the immigration systems of Canada and Australia. But both Canada and Australia admit *more* immigrants relative to the size of their population than the United States does. Cotton, Perdue, and Trump want to slash immigration levels by 50 percent, imposing an extremely stingy overall cap on the number of visas issued.

That means that lots of people who, by RAISE's own logic, count as highly meritorious—young, educated, English-speaking people with job offers that pay well above the state median income—are going to be locked out of the ability to immigrate to the United States. This makes sense if you think the US population is growing too robustly and it's important for us to try to fall behind China and India more quickly. Expert modelers calculate that under this system the total size of the American economy would be about 2 percent smaller by 2040 than it is under current policies—moving us in the exact opposite direction from where we should be trying to go.[*]

More realistically, the motive seems to be some nameless, unarticulated fear that it's simply bad to let foreigners move here.

Within that framework, one has to admit that it is reasonably well designed to minimize the damage to the American economy of sharply reducing immigration levels. On a *per person* basis, after all, GDP falls by just 0.3 percent.

But why, other than xenophobia and racism, would we want to adopt a policy shift that denies opportunities to foreigners at the

---

[*]Penn-Wharton Budget Model, "The RAISE Act: Effect on Economic Growth and Jobs," University of Pennsylvania, August 10, 2017, https://budgetmodel.wharton.upenn.edu/issues /2017/8/8/the-raise-act-effect-on-economic-growth-and-jobs.

cost of making native-born Americans slightly poorer and the country as a whole appreciably smaller and weaker?

You can see the fundamentally paranoid worldview underlying RAISE in some of the more eccentric choices surrounding point allocation.

A Nobel Prize winner, for example, gets 25 points (which is a lot) but only if it was received "in a field of scientific or social scientific study." In other words, winners of the Peace or Literature prizes don't qualify. But is it really reasonable to worry that our country is going to be overrun by foreign-born widely recognized literary geniuses? That they are going to put some kind of undue burden on the country's stock of hardworking native-born novelists and poets? The logic that scientific research has positive social externalities that don't necessarily exist in the literary field is, at a minimum, comprehensible. But the worldview that treats this as a concern is kind of baffling.

Kazuo Ishiguro, for example, would get 5 points for his foreign bachelor's degree and 12 points for his fluent command of English but be stuck with zero age points thanks to being older than fifty. Consequently, his eligibility to even *apply* for a visa by accruing 30 points would hinge on maxing out the income score by getting an annual salary offer that's worth more than 300 percent of the median household income in the state where the job is offered. My strong guess is that he could pull it off—the man has a Nobel Prize in Literature, after all—but if for whatever reason an internationally acclaimed Japanese-born British novelist with a Nobel Prize decided he wanted to take a $225,000-a-year job teaching creative writing at Johns

Hopkins, why on earth should we turn him down just because the job doesn't pay $240,000 a year or more?

Milwaukee Bucks star Giannis Antetokounmpo, similarly, might have been the 2018–19 season's Most Valuable Player, but because he's under twenty-six, he gets 8 age points rather than 10. He has little formal education, and income points max out at 13 for achieving more than 300 percent of Wisconsin's median household income (never mind that he earns far more than that). This makes his eligibility to apply for a visa entirely contingent on whether he can make it into the top 30 percent of the Test of English as a Foreign Language (TOEFL) scores, something that is not really relevant to his actual ability to succeed in the American labor market.

You might think he has a chance to sneak his way in through the provision granting 15 points to Olympic medal winners, but it needs to be in an *individual* sport—saving the United States from the specter of being overrun by foreign-born water polo players.

These are slightly fanciful edge cases, but they do underscore the extent to which RAISE offers a cramped and crabby view of what merit looks like. English language ability is, in fact, an important overall predictor of labor market success in the United States. But if you are a young person who is able to get a high-paying job offer despite weak English skills, there is probably some wisdom to the market's verdict that is not improved upon by Donald Trump playing language school central planner. Besides which, people's English skills predictably improve upon actually living and working here.

The United States really does allow some immigration as an act of charity. It would be, in my view, morally scandalous to not allow refugees into a country that has always defined itself as a haven for people in need. But refugees are selected for the amount of help they need, not for the amount of help they provide to us. So imposing quantitative limits on the number of cases we're willing to take on is perfectly reasonable—it's simply a question of exactly how stingy or kindhearted we would like to be.

But the bulk of immigration is beneficial to the interests of native-born Americans, and the existence of a strong flow of immigrants is beneficial to America's overall quest for strength and stature in the world. To the extent that we think we can do a better job of targeting individuals who are likely to be solid contributors, then we should seize the opportunity to recruit *more* of them rather than trying to get by with the bare minimum of possible immigrants. Could the country, for example, really find itself saddled with too many qualified medical professionals?

## Immigration could help fix health care

Opening the country to imported goods from abroad can help consumers get cheaper things, but can also cost manufacturing workers good-paying jobs.

Over the years, the United States has opted for a lot of openness to imported manufactured goods, and it has brought roughly the same benefits and costs that you would expect based on abstract theory. The unfortunate reality of this trade-off, however, is that at this point in American history relatively few Americans struggle to afford manufactured goods. Even low-income households in twenty-first-century America generally have televisions and mobile phones that would have dazzled their predecessors of a generation or two ago. We have lots of cars and household appliances.

But many Americans *do* struggle with the cost of health care. And even if the health-care system is substantially overhauled in ways that are designed to take those costs off the backs of patients, they will simply recur again as costs to the taxpayer. Finding ways to reduce those costs would be highly desirable.

And as it happens, foreign doctors seem to produce medical care at much lower costs. According to data from the Organization of Economic Co-operation and Development (OECD), American doctors earn more than their counterparts in any country other than perhaps Iceland.[*] We cannot, of course, really "trade" internationally in order to take advantage of cheap Canadian or German medical care in the same way that we can import iPhones from China. But we could allow competent foreign doctors to move here to work.

There are, of course, many foreign-born doctors in the United States. But their ability to practice is strictly limited.

As Dean Baker, the idiosyncratic left-wing economist who's been writing about this issue for years explains, "Currently, foreign doctors are banned from practicing unless they complete a U.S. residency program. Foreign dentists are prohibited from practicing in the United States unless they graduate from a U.S. dental school."

---

[*]See "Remuneration of Health Care Professionals," OECD, https://stats.oecd.org/Index.aspx?DataSetCode=HEALTH_REAC.

You obviously wouldn't want just any random graduate of any putative medical school in the world to come here and start doing brain surgery. But just as cars can be manufactured anywhere in the world as long as they follow Department of Transportation safety rules, a sensible approach would be to establish some clear objective training standards and then allow anyone who can meet them to practice in the United States. Indeed, faced with a critical shortage of medical personnel during the COVID-19 crisis, New York governor Andrew Cuomo temporarily waived the rules restricting foreign doctors—implicitly recognizing that the rules are not really necessary. Immigrant doctors might end up undercutting the salaries of native-born doctors, which would be a boon to the vast majority of Americans. And even if they didn't, simply increasing the supply of doctors would make getting treatment easier and more convenient for everyone—a clear win.

Meanwhile, even if immigrant doctors and dentists did earn somewhat less than today's American doctors and dentists, it's not like they'd be destitute, living in the streets, and collecting food stamps. They'd be paying taxes and supporting local businesses with their spending the same as any other upscale professionals.

Under the current immigration politics paradigm in the United States, any proposal to create a large new category of easy-to-obtain visas for foreign medical professionals would have to be offset by reducing some other category by a proportionate number. Because whatever category you pick would have its own constituency—and because some American doctors wouldn't like the idea—it would inevitably end up dying on the vine.

Once you accept the desirability of population growth, new vistas open up. A program allowing the importation of a large number of qualified foreign doctors and dentists is a good idea—so let's just make one.

## Immigrants and the welfare state

The last major concern about immigration is the idea that immigrants are a drain on the welfare state.

Indeed, in political terms this may be *the* key conceit driving contemporary anti-immigrant movements on the right across the developed world. In country after country, older working-class voters have been persuaded to flip allegiances away from left-of-center parties to right-wing anti-immigrant ones. That's in part based on dislike of the immigrants themselves. But it's also in part based on the idea that retirement and other social assistance programs are threatened not by conservative ties to the business community and the wealthy but by left-wing love of immigrants.

This, as we will see, is not factually accurate.

But it accords with the well-known phenomenon of "welfare chauvinism," the tendency of voters to be more supportive of a social safety net if they believe it will go to help people with whom they feel ethnic affinity. A study by Heather Hahn and others at the Urban Institute found, for example, that all else being equal, states with larger African American populations have less generous and more restrictive TANF (Temporary Assistance for Needy Families) policies.[*] Alberto Alesina and Ed Glaeser, in their own research on the interplay between racial diversity and the welfare state, recount that "in the 1880s, the first national pro-redistribution party—the Populists—rose in America. This group sought support from African-Americans who would particularly benefit from its policies. In response, conservative Whites spread stories emphasizing Black crimes and stoked the fires of racial hatred."[†]

In related research, Donald Kinder and Cindy Kam find that, among white voters, what they call ethnocentric attitudes have a strong negative correlation with support for means-tested social safety net programs but a strong *positive* correlation with support for Social Security and Medicare.[‡]

White voters, in short, conceptualize means-tested programs such as SNAP (food stamps), Medicaid, Section 8 housing vouchers, and TANF (welfare) as benefiting nonwhites, whereas Social Security and Medicare are seen as programs for them. Consequently, whites with more in-group loyalty are unusually hostile to the means-tested programs and unusually friendly to the universal ones.

Highly ethnocentric whites are, of course, also likely to oppose immigration.

---

[*]Heather Hahn et al., "Why Does Cash Welfare Depend on Where You Live?" Urban Institute, June 5, 2017, www.urban.org/research/publication/why-does-cash-welfare-depend-where-you-live.

[†]Alberto Alesina and Edward L. Glaeser, "Why Are Welfare States in the US and Europe So Different?" Horizons Stratégiques, 2006.

[‡]Donald Kinder and Cindy Kam, *Us Against Them: Ethnocentric Foundations of American Opinion* (Chicago: University of Chicago Press, 2010), tables 9.1 and 9.2.

Thus it would be convenient for the internal coherence of the ethnocentric white worldview if I were to say something like "Immigrants' heavy use of welfare programs is draining the government of revenue it needs to fund Social Security and Medicare for our seniors." Donald Trump took this a step further on the 2016 campaign trail claiming, falsely, that "our veterans, in many cases, are being treated worse than illegal immigrants."[*]

That absurd assertion aside, the basic finding of a comprehensive inquiry from the National Academy of Sciences is that immigration is on balance a net *positive* for the federal budget, largely due to the strong positive impact made by the children of immigrants.[†] As for immigrants themselves, there is quite a bit of variation with younger and better-educated immigrants tending to make a positive contribution, whereas older and less-educated immigrants end up imposing net costs—though even here, if they have kids, that makes up the gap.

The basic current situation, in short, is essentially fine.

But in the context of efforts to significantly expand immigration to the United States, it would be reasonable to make changes aimed at improving the fiscal deal for the country. The National Academy's survey is mostly a backward look at a period when the overall education level of immigrants to the United States was fairly low. Recent

---

[*]Michelle Ye He Lee, "Trump's ridiculous claim that veterans are 'treated worse' than undocumented immigrants," *Washington Post*, September 13, 2016.

[†]Francine D. Blau and Christopher Mackie, "The Economic and Fiscal Consequences of Immigration" (Washington, DC: The National Academies Press, 2017), 7.

immigrants are better educated; among new arrivals the share with a college degree is comparable to the native-born population, and the share with advanced degrees is higher.[*]

This is a trend that policy makers should try to continue as they expand immigration. The overall RAISE proposal is severely flawed, but the general idea of selecting for younger, better-educated immigrants with well-paying job offers makes sense. The medical visas concept I sketched earlier also has this property, as do the other main immigration ideas I'll discuss in this book.

Another idea that might be attractive in some contexts would be to make immigrants pay higher payroll taxes than natives. This sounds a bit harsh in some respects. The federal government normally taxes low-income households quite lightly for some fairly obvious moral reasons. But it's worth considering because the best available evidence suggests that low-skilled immigrants from poor countries can increase their incomes by huge amounts—the range varies considerably depending on which country we're talking about, but on average the increase is about fourfold—by moving to the United States.[†] Under the circumstances, any steps to actually cut back on the number of less-skilled immigrants who can come here would be extremely costly to some very needy people. If tax changes that make immigration slightly less economically favorable to the

[*]Jens Manuel Krogstad and Jynnah Radford, "Education levels of US immigrants are on the rise," Pew Center, September 14, 2018, www.pewresearch.org/fact-tank/2018/09/14/education-levels-of-u-s-immigrants-are-on-the-rise.

[†]Michael Clemens, Claudio Montenegro, and Lant Pritchett, "The Place Premium: Wage Differences for Identical Workers Across the US Border," HKS Faculty Research Working Paper Series, 2009.

migrants are what it takes to sustain political support for a high level of immigration, that would be a swap worth making.

Fundamentally, however, the details of optimal immigration policy design should be seen as essentially about political pragmatism rather than a need to design a truly optimal system.

# The path to citizenship

The one area where a specific choice is truly essential is the long-discussed, much-delayed concept of legal status and a path to citizenship for the bulk of the millions of unauthorized immigrants who've been living peacefully in the United States for years. It is not a good idea for a country to have millions of people living and working illegally within its borders. The country made a serious mistake back in the mid-1990s when, in response to concerns about illegal immigration, we made it much harder to cross the border and much harder for unauthorized residents to "get legal" without really addressing the ease with which employers could hire illegal workers without consequence.[*]

This was supposed to stop people from coming, but it didn't. Generally before the legal changes, people who came illegally would either go back home or else leverage US-citizen spouses or children into obtaining legal status, but now it was dangerous to rotate

---

[*]Dara Lind, "The Disastrous, Forgotten 1996 Law That Created Today's Immigration Problem," *Vox*, April 28, 2016, www.vox.com/2016/4/28/11515132/iirira-clinton-immigration.

between countries and impossible for people who'd arrived illegally to adjust their status.

As a result, new people came and simply stayed.

If it were possible to wave a magic wand and make this population of millions disappear instantly, the result would be an approximately 3 percent fall in the US population and a bigger drop in the size of the workforce. It would be, in other words, totally counterproductive to goals of national strength and growth.

And, of course, there is no magic wand at hand. Instead, the current policy approach is to immiserate and terrify millions of people while laboriously deporting a few hundred thousand of them each year at great expense. This is a cruel and pointless waste of resources. A far better approach, as embodied in the immigration reform legislation that passed the senate in 2013 only to die due to the opposition of House Republicans, is to give the vast majority of these people the opportunity to come forward, pay a fine, and get a visa.

This would be constructive for the American economy as newly legalized workers could get bank accounts and loans, save money and start businesses, and generally increase their level of contribution to the country. It would also detoxify immigration enforcement, getting activists off the backs of ICE agents so they could more safely apprehend a much smaller population of genuine bad actors.

People have reason to want a secure border and a controlled flow of migrants, but over the past decade the unauthorized population has been steadily dropping, and the border is essentially secure. A speedy grant of legal status can and should be paired with more aggressive measures to mandate the use of the E-Verify system so it's harder for people to fake their way into illegal jobs and to impose much tougher penalties on employers who break the rules.

But the failure of the 2013 reform bill was a fundamentally tragic turn that set much of American politics on a bad course. The one upside to the Trump administration's broad crackdown on *legal* immigration is that it's revealed the fundamental fakery that's been behind the opposition to that proposal all along—some people just plain don't like foreigners and don't want them to come here and are indifferent to the basic facts about economics and the logic of international power. We should not, as a country, follow their lead. And once we decide not to, a path to citizenship becomes a no-brainer.

## Climate and immigration

Contemporary criticism of immigration comes mostly from the same circles who deny that climate change is a problem at all, but it is worth saying that immigration to the United States raises greenhouse gas emissions through two channels. The first, which is plainly irrelevant, is that every time a person moves from Haiti to the United States, US emissions rise mechanically because we now have more people. This is true as an accounting matter but it has no relevance to the global climate problem.

What is relevant is that Haitians who move to the United States are much less poor than the ones who live in Haiti. Michael Clemens and Lant Pritchett studied this in detail and found that if you set the global poverty rate at an income of $10 per day, then "four out of five

Haitians who have escaped poverty by this global standard have done so in the US."* This poverty reduction does, however, entail greater emissions and exacerbates the climate change problem.

By the same token, the fact that contemporary Chinese people are no longer nearly as poor as Haitians accounts for the fact that Chinese emissions have soared.

The question here is whether it makes any kind of sense to try to keep people trapped in desperate poverty as an emissions reduction strategy. One problem is that it obviously won't work in general. Poor countries like India, Vietnam, and Ethiopia that have basically functional governments aren't going to voluntarily stay poor. Even so, many countries that don't want to be poor will probably continue to be poor for the foreseeable future anyway. We could contribute to their population's impoverishment by barring all immigration and tell ourselves we're striking a blow for environmental justice.

But that's perverse. And it's a lot closer to a right-wing caricature of what progressives think about climate change than to any sensible person's actual view of the issue.

Keeping poor people trapped in poor countries is the demographic equivalent of regressing to sailboat technology—a pseudosolution that can't possibly serve as the basis of global policy. On the contrary, letting people move should be part of the solution to coping with the realities of a changing climate.

---

*Michael Clemens and Lant Pritchett, "Income Per Natural: Measuring development as if people mattered more than places." Center for Global Development working paper, March 2008.

# Migration makes adaptation easier

Climate change is a global problem, but it doesn't affect the whole world the same way. Rising sea levels are an acute problem for low-lying coastal population centers but not a big deal for places that are farther inland. Small islands are much more threatened than large landmasses. The increased warmth on its own terms will significantly increase the number of people exposed to potentially lethal heat conditions across significant swaths of the world. But people living in cold places today are exposed to potentially lethal freezing conditions that will become rarer. Crop yields will decline in many parts of the world, but they will rise in others.

By all scientific accounts the net impact of these changes will be negative—and not in a small way. One important reason is that the global population is not distributed randomly around the world. There are more people living in tiny and extremely vulnerable Bangladesh than in all of Russia, and more people in Nigeria than in Russia and Canada combined. So potentially improved conditions in the vast landmasses of the north don't really "offset" acute problems in the tropics to any reasonable degree.

But the extent to which offsetting happens or not hinges crucially on the extent to which global migration is allowed.

The United States is not going to be spared the negative impacts of climate change—already we see wildfires worsening in California and increased river flooding in the Midwest, while rising sea levels will challenge Florida and Eastern Seaboard cities. But in the grand scheme of things we are better situated than many other countries. Americans are not peasant farmers whose livelihoods are closely tied to the vagaries of the weather. Defending New York and Boston from coastal flooding will be expensive, but it's certainly feasible. And much of America is cold enough that it will likely see some upside from warming. There's no reason to think Buffalo, Worcester, Chicago, or Minneapolis are poised to become particularly hazardous or unpleasant places to live. If people were able to magically relocate themselves, climate change wouldn't be nearly as big a problem.

Klaus Desmet and Esteban Rossi-Hansberg are scholars focused on the economics of place and space who've spent years pushing for more attention to be paid to this reality.

"The negative economic effects of climate change are likely to stem predominantly from frictions—that is, national borders—that prevent the free movement of people and goods," they wrote in a 2013 paper.* In a 2015 follow-up they make the further observation that, examined globally, 75 percent of the human population and 91 percent of economic output come from just 10 percent of the total landmass. Under the circumstances, "If we expect large economic losses from global warming, those cannot come just from the direct effect of temperature increases on the productivity of land."†

That's not to trivialize the very real problems here. You can't just pick up Miami and move it to the middle of Nebraska. Finding ways

---

*Klaus Desmet and Esteban Rossi-Hansberg, "Moving to Greenland in the Face of Global Warming," *VoxEU*, January 16, 2013, https://voxeu.org/article/moving-greenland-face-global -warming.

†Klaus Desmet and Esteban Rossi-Hansberg, "On the Spatial Economic Impact of Global Warming," *Journal of Urban Economics*, May 15, 2015.

to minimize the actual extent of warming will have very large benefits. But the fact remains that reducing barriers to population movement is a highly effective way of reducing warming's costs. Just as on the emissions-reduction question, the United States does not hold the destiny of the entire world in its hands alone here. The future of migration to other Northern Hemisphere countries, and especially Canada and Russia, is very important. But as I've argued from the beginning, the United States is a very large and sparsely populated country with plenty of fresh water and agricultural land.

Some of our territory is highly vulnerable to climate change, but much of it is scarcely populated because people find it to be unpleasantly cold. The billion Americans agenda here is very clearly in line with the imperative to contribute to global climate change adaptation.

## More people, more ideas

But beyond adapting to climate change, to halt its advance we need to invent some better technologies.

Right now there are no viable substitutes for fossil fuels at hand for applications like air travel, maritime shipping, a range of industrial and agricultural applications, and many categories of heavy equipment. Trying to cut down on unnecessary consumption of these carbon-intensive commodities is useful and admirable. But fundamentally, people aren't going to give up on long-distance travel and shipping. We need to invent some better stuff—new ways of doing those things or new kinds of cost-effective carbon scrubbers.

There's no great "invent new stuff" button that policy makers can press. What they *can* do is invest in both targeted R&D and basic science paired with a commitment to spend meaningful money on early deployment so that engineers can learn by doing.

But it also stands to reason that a nation of 1 billion Americans will invent more useful new technologies than a nation of 330 million Americans. A parent of three children is more likely to see a child grow up to be a major inventor than a parent of one. That's just math.

"If there's less population growth, there's less growth in the number of people to do research," observes Stanford University economist Peter Klenow, who's grown concerned that the slowing US population growth rate is related to the slowdown in productivity growth.*

Immigrants, in particular, have been major drivers of innovation in the United States. Immigrants are responsible for about 28 percent of high-quality patents filed in the United States, are disproportionately represented among America's science Nobel Prize winners, and slightly more than half of America's high-growth start-ups have at least one immigrant founder.

Foreigners would like to move here because the economic opportunities that exist in the United States are superior to what they would find in the vast majority of the world. We have a better-

---

*James Pethokoukis, "How will America's economy grow in the 2020s? My long-read Q&A with Peter Klenow," American Enterprise Institute, January 16, 2020, www.aei.org/tech nology-and-innovation/how-will-americas-economy-grow-in-the-2020s-a-long-read-qa -with-peter-klenow.

functioning legal system, democratic politics, plenty of rich investors and middle-class customers, and living standards that are generally much higher than what's found in Nicaragua, Nigeria, or Nepal. A family who moves here is much less likely to see their kids be malnourished or deprived of basic schooling, and they are consequently much more likely to grow up to innovate and change the world in major ways.

The fact that modern living standards are driven primarily by innovation rather than natural resources is the fundamental reason that population growth increases rather than reduces prosperity. The climate problem raises the stakes but doesn't fundamentally alter the calculus. The progress that *has* been made on reducing emissions in the United States and Europe has come overwhelmingly through the creation and deployment of new and better technologies. Future progress hinges on generating more of the same—but also on spreading the progress globally so that poor and middle-income countries can get richer and cleaner simultaneously.

And an influx of new people brings with them not just new ideas but also the possibility of revitalizing the large swaths of the country that are endowed with strong fundamentals but have lost much of their population.

# CHAPTER 6

# Comeback Cities

The story of Amazon's quest to build an office facility it initially dubbed HQ2 is one of the most depressing that I've ever covered. It announced with great fanfare a nationwide search for a second headquarters featuring tens of thousands of jobs. Ultimately it chose to create two new large satellite office campuses, one in Queens and one in the suburbs of Washington, DC. Then the Queens, New York, plan was scuttled by local political opposition, ostensibly about the tax abatements that had been offered to sweeten the deal but on some level more broadly because a lot of political stakeholders in the neighborhood didn't actually *want* a big new office complex there.

Arlington County in Virginia, by contrast, was happy to get one—largely because the place where Amazon is setting up shop had become a semi-abandoned office complex after the 2005 Base Realignment and Closure (BRAC) process moved a lot of Defense Department jobs out of the area.

The striking thing about Arlington is that the loss of those Defense jobs, though it had left the Crystal City office district as something of a ghost town, was hardly devastating to the county's larger well-being. It simply continued to be a rich, expensive suburb of Washington, DC, with some vacant office buildings. Had Amazon not come along, new commercial tenants would probably have emerged in the longer term. And given the generally high price of housing in the region, it's a given that the area could have been rezoned for residential construction and attracted many new residents. Arlington preferred to win the marquee Amazon prize, but it hardly needed it.

While the project will bring a lot of new construction and office jobs to the county, it very much isn't the centerpiece of a larger agenda of transformation. In particular, there are few plans to rezone the adjacent single-family neighborhood (or any other neighborhood in the county) for higher density. The influx of jobs will not be paired with a commensurate influx of new homes and residents. Instead, regional housing prices will be pushed further up. Skilled workers able to get high-paying jobs at Amazon (or to bargain for higher pay at their current employer, thanks to the competition) will come out ahead. So will people who already own a home that's a convenient commute from the new Amazon office. But working-class renters will get the short end of the stick.

This is the tragedy of HQ2, not the overly debated issue of tax subsidies but the selection of locations that didn't really need a big new Amazon office—to the point where one of them ended up telling Amazon to buzz off.

Early in the selection process there had been a lot of hype around bids made by smaller cities, midwestern cities, and cities desperate for an economic shot in the arm. Those choices would have been more exciting for journalists and better for America. But Amazon is, obviously, a for-profit business that is trying to make decisions that make business sense. And while I wasn't happy with the outcome of the selection process, I don't think Amazon's business logic was mistaken.

Building a bigger America will mean finding ways to fit more people into our most crowded and expensive cities. These are the places where the job opportunities are most plentiful and where additional people could be most economically valuable—if we could unlock the potential for more growth.

But a strategy for national growth can't just involve cramming more and more people into New York, San Francisco, and Seattle.

One of the great tragedies of contemporary American life is that we have several major cities—and dozens of smaller ones—slowly wasting away due to population decline. These cities all have their share of real problems, but what place doesn't? Fundamentally, in most of the ways that matter, Detroit, St. Louis, Cleveland, Milwaukee, Buffalo, and the rest are great places to live.

But they suffer from two key flaws. One is that they're cold. Cold isn't the end of the world for a city—Boston, Minneapolis, and Stockholm are all thriving—but all else being equal, people tend to move toward warmer places.* The other flaw is that they are losing people in large part because they are losing people.

Shrinking cities offer a worse balance of taxes to services than growing ones because today's smaller population needs to pay pension obligations incurred by yesterday's larger ones. They don't attract investment because they are shrinking and don't need many new buildings. The lack of new investment creates a lack of job opportunities, which encourages further shrinkage.

The result is a slow, steady deterioration of the shrinking cities' unique cultural assets and lifestyle amenities. That encourages further shrinkage and the wasting away of much of the cities' potential. Any reasonable strategy for national renewal needs to place a high priority on doing what we reasonably can to spread economic opportunity away from the places that are suffering from housing shortages and toward the places that are suffering from a dearth of investment.

## Hollowed-out cities

The story of Detroit's decline from high-tech industrial hub of the mid-twentieth century to its current post-bankruptcy, crime-ridden shell of its former self is infamous with "ruin porn" of abandoned buildings easy to find on the internet.

But what's even more shocking than Detroit's decline from 1.85 million people to about 380,000 is that in percentage terms it isn't

---

*Edward L. Glaeser, "Reinventing Boston: 1630–2003," *Journal of Economic Geography*, 2005.

even the biggest drop among American cities. That honor belongs to St. Louis, which has lost 65 percent of the 856,000 residents it had in 1950, when it was the eighth largest city in the country.

And other declines, though not quite as dramatic in percentage terms, are still staggering in scope. Philadelphia has lost "only" 25 percent of its peak population, but that still amounts to 500,000 people. Cleveland has also lost half a million. Baltimore has lost 350,000 people, and Buffalo has lost nearly as many. New Orleans and Pittsburgh are down nearly 250,000 people. Cincinnati has lost 200,000. Newark and Milwaukee have lost about 150,000. Toledo, Akron, Rochester, Syracuse, and Gary have lost about 100,000 each. Providence has lost a mere 74,000. And there's a long tail of small northeastern cities that were never particularly large to begin with that have lost a few tens of thousands of people each—Hartford, Bridgeport, and New Haven in Connecticut; Springfield, Worcester, and Fall River in Massachusetts; Bangor and Lewiston in Maine; Utica and Rome in New York; Erie, Reading, and Harrisburg in Pennsylvania; Camden, Trenton, and Atlantic City in New Jersey.

In parts of the Midwest things are, if anything, worse. Five out of Michigan's ten most populated municipalities are shrinking. It's six out of ten in Ohio.

These hollow cities are worth paying attention to in part simply to establish the point that there is plenty of space in the country for extra people—many of them could go smack dab in the middle of our historic cities without any problem at all—but also because they illustrate something fundamental about the social and economic dynamics of population growth.

Humanity spent most of its existence in hunter-gatherer bands or engaged in subsistence agriculture. When wealth derived from the land, fewer people meant more wealth. A tragedy like the Black Death was a boon to survivors, significantly increasing wages in England even though there was no underlying improvement in agricultural productivity.* Conversely, superficially good practices like superior hygiene in East Asia resulting in persistently lower rates of death by infectious disease created persistently lower living standards.† These kinds of intuitions are deeply embedded in our psychology, and often excessively color discussions of population growth—particularly ones that muddy the waters between developing countries, where a huge share of the population is still engaged in subsistence agriculture, and modern technologically advanced service economies.

But despite these intuitions, everyone recognizes that precipitous population decline has done the cities of the American rust belt no favors.

The original impulses for population decline were external. The invention of the automobile made it possible and in many cases desirable to live outside of the central city. Racism and fear of crime provided further impetus for white flight. Then for midwestern cities, deindustrialization provided a huge additional economic blow. At this point, however, population loss is not just a consequence of

---

*Gregory Clark, "Microbes and Markets: Was the Black Death an Economic Revolution?" *Journal of Demographic Economics* 82, no. 2, June 2016, 139–65, https://doi.org/10.1017/dem.2016.6. For an even more optimistic account, see Peter Temin, "The Black Death and Industrialization: Lessons for Today's South," *VoxEU*, June 4, 2014, https://voxeu.org/article/economic-history-and-economic-development.

†Gregory Clark, *A Farewell to Alms* (Princeton, NJ: Princeton University Press, 2007), 106–107.

external problems; it's become its own self-sustaining source of difficulty. The residents of Detroit and other shrunken cities are not farmers who are able to take over their neighbors' vacated land and exploit it to raise their living standards. On the contrary, a shrunken city means a shrunken tax base so the quality of city services declines—especially considering the need to keep making payments on old pension obligations.

Fewer residents also means fewer customers for neighborhood-based service businesses. That means fewer options for the remaining residents, depriving city living of one of its main attractions. But in part because of the lack of public service funding, several of the major reasons to *avoid* city living—crime and concern about the schools—become only more intense. The main virtue of the depopulating city is that houses there are cheaper than in more desirable places. But that sets in motion a negative selection—the only people sticking around are those without the means to leave, a population that also lacks the means to pay taxes and support local businesses.

Soon enough, the cheapness of the houses itself becomes a liability. As Issi Romem, the chief economist of BuildZoom has noted, in many of these declining cities the purchase price of a building is lower than the replacement cost of rebuilding that same structure in place.[*]

That's why these cities are cursed with derelict structures and abandoned buildings that become eyesores and havens for literal vermin.

But the impact on nonvacant structures, though harder to see,

---

[*]Issi Romem, "Paying for Dirt," BuildZoom, October 17, 2017, www.buildzoom.com/blog/paying-for-dirt-where-have-home-values-detached-from-construction-costs.

is insidious as well. A landlord whose property is worth less at sale than its replacement value has no incentive to do proper upkeep on his buildings. Tenants will get, at best, what they are legally entitled to and realistically less than that because enforcement is spotty. That means inadequate heat in the winter, grim conditions all year round, and often legitimately dangerous problems of mold and rodents. The vicious, purely extractive relationship between landlord and tenant in Milwaukee that Matthew Desmond so expertly describes in his Pulitzer Prize-winning book, *Evicted*, is in part a consequence of this. Landlords in rapidly growing cities don't miraculously become selfless people, but they do safeguard the value of their investment in a way that Desmond's landlords don't. And in growing cities, people build new buildings to compete with the incumbents—which doesn't really happen when the existing buildings have so little value.

Homeowners, meanwhile, don't just abandon their property to blight and despair. They, after all, have to live there, so they do their best to keep things up.

But while homeowners in conventional growing cities see their "sweat equity" converted into actual monetary value, for homeowners in shrinking cities the effort—though not exactly wasted—has no real *financial* upside. The withering away of the city frustrates the best efforts of the most conscientious homeowners, bleeding their finances and encouraging further flight.

Which is to say that not only do America's hollow cities have plenty of room to accommodate more people, they and their existing stock of residents would benefit massively from repopulation, provided it could be done in a halfway intelligent manner. But under current policies, the problems are instead spreading out from the original focal points of the blight.

## Suburban shrinkage

The initial phase of urban decline can be thought of primarily as an adjustment to a technological shock. American cities were built around railroad stations, especially places where multiple train lines converged or where they intersected with useful rivers or ports.

In the heyday of urban America, as the Yale political scientist Douglas Rae writes, "The development of what will eventually be known as suburban sprawl was limited—less by taste or preference than by the absence of fast, flexible transportation capable of linking peripheral locations to the central city."* There was a huge economic premium on being located within a convenient walk or cart trip from a train station. Big cities would, of course, spread out somewhat along the lines of a mass transit network. But smaller cities would simply cluster around the main station and associated waterfront. Land was not objectively scarce but *access* to the main features of the city was.

The automobile changed that in the 1920s, but the transformation was halted by fifteen years of depression and war that suppressed car buying and home building.

In the postwar years, the new technology exploded. Because it was now possible to get downtown without living close to downtown,

---

*Douglas Rae, *City: Urbanism and Its End* (New Haven, CT: Yale University Press, 2003), 11.

millions of Americans chose to do so, and the population of the suburbs exploded even faster than the overall population of the United States—even though in this baby boom era the population was growing quite rapidly.

Today, of course, there are still rapidly growing suburbs, especially in the booming metro areas of the sun belt. But not only has the City of Chicago been losing population in recent years, so is Cook County overall, as well as the inner-ring suburbs of DuPage and Lake Counties.* Another Lake County—the one in Indiana—is also part of the Chicago suburbs, and it's also shrinking. Allegheny County, which contains Pittsburgh and some surrounding suburbs, is shrinking. But so are five out of six other counties that make up the Pittsburgh Metropolitan Statistical Area. The City of St. Louis is shrinking, as are several of the counties in its suburbs.

Local circumstances vary from place to place, but the overall pattern has a simple basic logic to it.

Suburban living has considerable charms, but in general you'd rather live in a suburb of a healthy and thriving city with interesting things to do on the occasional weekend trip and some major employment anchors. In a booming metro area like Washington, DC, new arrivals to the suburbs have often decamped from the central city—generally with a toddler in tow and perhaps a second child on the way. But if the center city doesn't attract young singles, there's no

---

*John Pletz, "Chicago Is Still Losing Population," *Crain's Chicago Business*, April 17, 2019.

one to get married and move out to the suburbs for the sake of the schools or a bigger yard.

What's more, while we don't have a great deal of experience with suburban population decline, there is reason to believe that once it sets in, it may be an even tougher cycle to escape than the urban variant. Even the most troubled central cities, after all, tend to retain a number of unique cultural and civic assets along with government offices and other enduring sources of employment. They are advantaged by legacy transportation infrastructure that makes their downtowns a logical place to put things. And some of their taxable assets like hotels and bars can be fairly indifferent to the actual quality of municipal public service provision.

Suburbs, by comparison, tend to be poorly differentiated. If a given place's tax base begins to erode due to population loss, forcing higher rates to maintain equal service quality, there is relatively little to stop additional people from moving away in search of a better value proposition.

Historically this vulnerability to population loss has actually been a major source of strength for American suburbs. The mechanism is what's known to specialists as Tiebout competition— essentially people voting with their feet to live in jurisdictions that do a good job of spending tax revenue in cost-effective ways. Because city officials, municipal workers, and local businesses all have a strong interest in avoiding population loss, the key interest groups are well aligned around the goal of aiming to set taxes at appropriate levels and spend money on things people actually value. Big cities, precisely because they have a more unique value proposition to offer, are less constrained and their leaders can often do well for themselves through malgovernment.*

But the underlying presumption here is that population loss would be the exception rather than the rule because *overall* populations are growing strongly. That was the case during the postwar years when Charles Tiebout originally published this model, and it could be again if America opted to change its policy trajectory. At the moment, however, overall population growth is extremely slow and trending downward with many current policy initiatives oriented toward pushing it even further down. And right now we have a situation where population decline is taking place across most of the country.

## Combatting rural shrinkage

A small town isn't a small town if it gets too big, and a rural county isn't rural anymore if too many people live there. Given the sense of threat and beseigement that preoccupies many rural communities these days there is naturally going to be some resistance to a message that is all about the virtues of bigness.

That said, on a practical level the amount of rural land that is

---

*David Schleicher, "The City as a Law and Economics Subject," *University of Illinois Law Review* 2010: 1508.

being absorbed into big metro areas (so-called sprawl) is relatively small compared with the amount that is simply being abandoned.

Right now 24 percent of all American counties, an overwhelmingly rural set, are depopulating. And there is a hard-core depopulation belt composing about a third of rural counties that currently have fewer residents than they had in 1950.*

To an extent, this makes the point that the country has plenty of room for more people. But depopulation is a huge practical problem because the trends that generate it can feed on themselves. When a town has too few kids to support a local elementary school, that makes it a less attractive place to live for young adults with kids. When they move away, the local store may close, which makes the town a less convenient place for everyone to live. Young people who, in principal, might like to live in their hometown see a lack of practical opportunity for them to get jobs and have things to do, and so they move away.

A particularly acute form of the depopulation spiral is seen in the wave of rural hospital closures the United States has experienced over the past decade. Some of this reflects foolish decision making like the tendency of Republican-dominated states to refuse Medicaid expansion, thus depriving their population of health care and their local providers of customers. But the broader trend is visible in both expansion and nonexpansion states.

---

*Kenneth Johnson and Daniel Lichter, "Rural Depopulation in a Rapidly Urbanizing America," University of New Hampshire Carsey School of Public Policy, February 6, 2019, https://carsey.unh.edu/publication/rural-depopulation.

And fundamentally that's no surprise. Hospitals have big fixed costs, and it's difficult to cover those costs in a place where not that many people live. This means that not only do many rural people need to travel inconveniently far to get medical care—the COVID-19 crisis revealed that many small rural hospitals have no intensive care facilities—there tend to be very low levels of competition and thus high costs. The situation with broadband internet is essentially the same—building these systems is very expensive, and companies aren't inclined to do it in a place where few people live. But high health-care costs and poor availability of modern communication technology encourage people to move away, which worsens the very problems that drove them to leave in the first place.

The most basic solution is to pony up more cash for subsidies. But that in turn is one way in which urban and rural fates are linked—bigger, richer metropolitan areas are more able to cross-subsidize all kinds of useful rural infrastructure.

But reversing rural depopulation would accomplish two useful things. One is simply that a given amount of subsidy would go further if rural populations were higher and rising, allowing subsidy programs to maximize their effectiveness. More important, all the fiber-optic cables and extra hospital reimbursements in the world can't make a thriving community. Only actual human inhabitants can do that. Lots of people prefer to live in places that aren't crowded, teeming cities. But nobody wants to live in places that are being steadily abandoned and transformed into naturally occurring retirement communities.

The basic tendency for young adults, on net, to tend to leave rural

areas for more excitement in urban ones has existed since time im-
memorial. Traditionally that's been offset by the fact that rural areas,
with more space and tighter-knit communities (and fewer infectious
diseases), are better optimized for raising families. A world in which
Americans writ large don't have the financial resources to have the
number of children they'd like deprives them of that advantage and
over time saps their vitality. The rise of central cities where dogs
outnumber children reflects policy failures, but urban areas do at
least function on a basic level as playgrounds for the childless while
rural ones simply end up denuded of people and basic services.

## Chicken and egg

The basic issue is that if you are a company like Amazon and you
want to establish a big new office full of well-paid white-collar professionals with college degrees, the best way to do it is to situate
yourself somewhere that is already populated with white-collar professionals with college degrees. In part this is for the obvious reason
that in a city full of college graduates, you can hire them.

But it's also easier to recruit new workers to move to a city that's
already full of white-collar professionals. Lots of Portland residents
who might consider a job opportunity in Austin or Boston would be
more reluctant to chase one in Tulsa or Toledo.

One reason is that people don't like to lock themselves in to
specific employers. A place full of educated professionals is, by definition, a place that has many different places where white-collar

professionals work. So if that new job in Austin doesn't work out or if candidates simply want the flexibility to make career moves during the years to come, there are probably more *other* opportunities there than in Toledo.

Many people have spouses. These days there's a phenomenon called assortative mating, which occurs when people choose partners similar to themselves—for example, college graduates tend to marry other college graduates. Given that, it's much easier for you to seize a new white-collar professional job opportunity if it's in a city where your spouse is likely to be able to find his own white-collar professional job opportunity.

If you're not married, meanwhile, then you'd like to move to a city with an appealing dating market. And here the same assortative logic applies. If you're a college graduate doing professional work, you'll find more eligible suitors in Boston than in Tulsa. For that matter, you're more likely to find platonic friends with whom you have things in common. And for basically similar reasons, there are likely to be more retail outlets that cater to your interests.

The result of this is that skilled professionals have strong incentives to move to metro areas that are already full of other skilled professionals. And employers of skilled professionals have strong incentives to locate in metro areas that are already full of other employers of skilled professionals. And the same dynamics make these cities the most promising places for start-ups.

If your city happens to be on the positive side of this dynamic, that's very good news for it. San Francisco manages to have a booming economy even though it's not by any conventional standard a particularly well-governed city. Taxes are high, the public schools aren't well regarded, and the mass transit is mediocre at best, even by American standards. But for a variety of contingent historical, geographic, and climactic reasons, it became a hub of skilled work and that hub is now self-sustaining. Cities that don't have that favorable history face a struggle.

## The growing divide

Some American cities, generally in the sun belt, are able to take advantage of warm weather, business-friendly state governments, and a lack of legacy pension obligations to at least get on a positive population growth trajectory. Many, many people move to metro areas like Atlanta, Charlotte, Dallas, and Phoenix, where low housing costs provide higher standards of living for working-class people than are achieved in the coastal metropolises. But wages and productivity remain stubbornly lower in these places than in the rich coastal metros.

One often hears that economic activity has become more concentrated in a handful of "superstar" cities. But as Jed Kolko, an economist specializing in urban labor markets who now works for the job site Indeed, has shown, this is a mistake. What's happening is that *average incomes* are becoming more unequal as superstar cities pull away from the pack. But because the superstar cities are growing so much slower than the power sun belt boomtowns, their share of overall national output isn't actually growing.

We have essentially two growth models. The superstar cities attract skilled workers from all around the country (and, indeed, the world) but then eject working-class residents due to housing scarcity. The sun belt cities attract more rapid population growth but have stagnant incomes because they can't attract elite employers.

This divergence trend is not ideal, but it's at least workable. But for colder cities that grew large around factories that later went into decline—and were often originally oriented around waterways and railroad connections that are no longer so economically relevant—the cycle is disastrous.

Every troubled American city has made its share of policy mistakes. And typically the state governments of places like Missouri, Wisconsin, and Michigan have underrated the long-term value to the state as a whole of investing in St. Louis, Milwaukee, and Detroit. But they're not fundamentally in trouble because of policy mistakes made at either the state or the local level. They're in trouble because the chicken-and-egg dynamics are just too hard to break.

Oftentimes market economies exhibit strong tendencies to return to equilibrium. If a sudden fad for eating beets makes beets scarce and expensive, farmers will plant more beets and they'll become affordable again.

In theory, cities could work like this too. Seattle is a great place to do business, but the Seattle metro area is on the small side to be host to two of the country's five most valuable companies. So even though the city has been growing fast, it's also become very expensive and is suffering from shortfalls in housing, office space, and transportation infrastructure. Cleveland, conversely, has an airport, three pro sports teams, a few excellent museums, a major orchestra, and a great theater district, but disinvestment has left it incredibly cheap. A convenient outcome for American society would be for the low price of Cleveland to attract investment, with various HQ2s or similar facilities replacing some of the surface parking lots that currently scar its downtown.

But in practice we've seen that it doesn't work that way.

Google's biggest office presence is in Silicon Valley, and its number two is in New York City. Amazon's big expansion is coming to the DC area. And when companies do reach outside the big coastal cities, they tend to find that the most attractive candidates are places like Nashville and Austin—state capitals with a strong university presence and hip cultural scene rather than shrinking rust belt metros. There's nothing wrong with Nashville and Austin. But to an extent, that's the problem. For free market equilibrium to save Cleveland, there would need to be something repelling corporate investment from the sun belt as well from as the expensive coastal cities.

That's just business. But for the country, it's a huge waste of potential.

The national media has gotten very interested in the pathologies of cities that have become too expensive. There is extensive, frequent coverage of the interlocking crises of affordability, homelessness, and gentrification in the big cities of the Northeast and the West Coast.

These are real problems (and we'll do a whole chapter on them) but they are more limited in their scale than a lot of media narratives suggest.

A larger set of cities is suffering from systematic disinvestment.

And their poor neighborhoods are suffering not from gentrification and displacement, but from the ongoing departure of people with the means to flee. That's what leads to metro areas where existing houses are worth less than what it would cost to build a brand-new one.

Affordability is good. But taken to this extreme it's a problem. It means that the time, money, and work that homeowners put into their houses largely waste rather than build wealth. And it means there's little opportunity for new construction to be viable, an often good reason for property owners to skimp on upkeep. The existing capital stock deteriorates and as the tax base erodes, so does the public infrastructure.

Harder to quantify but equally real is the deleterious impact on civic institutions. The most famous ones, such as the Detroit Institute of Arts or the Cleveland Orchestra, stay viable but end up underused relative to what they could be if the cities that surround them were larger and growing. Smaller museums and other donor-financed nonprofits may not be so lucky. And institutions like churches, clubs, and other voluntary organizations inevitably suffer from population flight because they are inherently powered by their memberships.

Broad background conditions of more rapid population growth can help cities suffering from a downward spiral of disinvestment and population loss. But concentrated relocation of reasonably well-paying jobs to such cities is an especially powerful tool. By simultaneously raising population and incomes, it can help raise land values back to the "normal" situation where building new structures (and keeping up existing ones) makes sense. That creates broad economic benefits—jobs in building trades, wealth-building for homeowners, a richer service economy—for people who wouldn't necessarily think of themselves as affected by relocations in a direct way.

The easiest and probably least controversial place to start would be with the federal government itself. The trick is to carry it out with a modicum of thoughtfulness.

# Decentralize the federal government

Most federal employees don't work in the Washington, DC, area.*

Of course many of them do. Oftentimes that's for a good specific reason. But sometimes it's just a legacy of tradition. With the communications and transportation technologies that existed decades ago, it was useful to concentrate essentially all agencies within the same city regardless of their specific function or purpose. And of course once a given agency is up and running in a particular place, it's a lot more convenient for everyone involved to keep it in the same general area forever.

And for a long time that system worked well enough, especially because DC had the reputation of being something of a backwater.

Today, though, the DC metro area is one of the largest in the

---

*Ed O'Keefe, "Where are most federal employees? Not in Washington," *Washington Post*, September 12, 2011.

country. And in per person terms, it's among the richest in the country. It's also one of the most expensive markets in which to rent office space.*

This means that for all the basic chicken-and-egg reasons discussed above, the Washington area doesn't really *need* the marginal federal job. If the Bureau of Engraving and Printing were to vanish from its two-building complex just south of the National Mall, there would be no problem finding alternate tenants for this valuable land in an expensive city. It could be commercial office space or perhaps a hotel. The federal government could raise some money by selling the structure, and the city would benefit from transforming it from nontaxable federal buildings into taxable privately owned ones. There are more than a thousand jobs associated with the BEP complex, but the DC area has a robust labor market and the people working there could likely find other work.

But ideally, many of the Bureau's current employees would simply follow it to a new home elsewhere. The DC housing market is incredibly expensive, so people leaving would simply relieve existing pressure. Prices would fall marginally, and the homes vacated would be filled with newcomers.

By contrast, downtown Youngstown, Ohio—like many other small American cities—has plenty of space for two additional big buildings. Housing in Youngstown is cheap, and buildable land is plentiful—there'd be no problem accommodating additional resi-

---

*Sarah Berger, "These Are the 10 Best Big Cities for Starting a Business in the US," CNBC, May 4, 2018, www.cnbc.com/2018/05/04/wallethub-survey-best-big-cities-to-start-a-business -in-america.html.

dents. In fact, it would be the opposite of a problem. Extra workers downtown would be extra customers for downtown businesses. Additional residents would strengthen the local tax base. You'd have fundamentally a win-win transaction by taking jobs out of a high-priced, overcrowded place and putting them into a cheap under-populated one.

And while you wouldn't want to send the State Department to Milwaukee, there are plenty of government functions that are more like those of the Bureau of Engraving and Printing. They're important but not, in a practical sense, enmeshed in day-to-day partisan politics, which, fundamentally, they shouldn't be. They are doing important work, but it's not work that requires agency leaders to have frequent face time with the president or be routinely available to members of Congress.

Shifting agencies like that away from the national capital region and to cities that have fallen far below their historical peak populations could pay considerable long-term dividends—allowing higher living standards for federal workers, freeing up space in a crowded and expensive city, and rescuing tons of private, public, and social capital from wastage and despair.

## Real plans, not culture war

When I wrote an article advocating the relocation of federal agencies to the Midwest in the winter of 2016–17, it struck me as far-fetched. Over the next couple of years, I was first heartened and then horrified to learn that the Trump administration was actually doing this with a bunch of US Department of Agriculture (USDA) personnel, and it was turning into a disaster.

USDA is a reasonable candidate for relocation both because its work is not super political and also because the DC area is quite remote from America's main agricultural areas.

But in practice, instead of being a modest but useful economic development scheme that allowed federal workers to obtain higher living standards, it played out as just another Trump-era culture war food fight. Agency personnel were given very little notice, planning time, or even clarity about where exactly in Missouri their jobs were being moved. There was a massive number of complaints, and the majority of the staff at the Economic Research Service and the National Institute of Food and Agriculture wound up quitting rather than relocating.

The perception in the policy community was that the Trump administration welcomed this brain drain as part of a larger assault on bureaucratic expertise in the administrative state.

"This is really about an attack on science," Rebecca Boehm of the Union of Concerned Scientists told NPR, "and an attack on agencies that produce objective research and information in the public interest."[*]

Following Boehm, progressives generally asserted that the entire relocation effort was a bad-faith initiative designed to destroy and

---

*Frank Morris, "Critics of Relocating USDA Research Agencies Point To Brain Drain," *All Things Considered*, September 10, 2019, www.npr.org/2019/09/10/759053717/critics-of -relocating-usda-research-agencies-point-to-brain-drain.

demobilize the agencies. When *Washington Post* columnist Greg Sargent tweeted some commentary along those lines, Missouri senator Josh Hawley—a graduate of Stanford and Yale Law School—fired back with a series of tweets slamming Sargent as a "smug, rich liberal elitist" who expressed "open contempt for the people of the heartland and all we love."[*]

That's good culture war politics from Hawley. But it's disastrous from the standpoint of actually trying to advance the cause of agency relocation—something that midwestern cities like the ones Hawley represents could really benefit from. You don't need to be smug or an elitist to have a problem with being told precipitously that your job is moving thousands of miles away. All you need is a spouse with a job of his own, a kid with friends and a school and a routine, or ties to your own social circle and community institutions. Politicians who understand why "just move somewhere else" isn't an adequate answer to residents of economically ailing regions should also understand why you can't just up and order people to leave Bethesda and move to Kansas City on the spur of the moment.

But a relocation plan that's universally despised is simply one that hasn't been designed in a very thoughtful manner.

As a known apologist for the DC metro area, I can confirm that relatively few of us who live here came for the scenic views (no mountains, no ocean, no big lakes) or the weather (months of brutal humidity). We moved here for work. The region has a lot of

---

[*]Ed Kilgore, "Smug, Elitist Senator Attacks Middle-Class Journalist as a Smug Elitist," *New York*, October 22, 2019, http://nymag.com/intelligencer/2019/10/smug-elitist-senator-hawley-attacks-humble-journalist.html.

specialized government-related employment opportunities and a generally strong economy. But it's also on the expensive side. Like most people who live here, I couldn't really pursue my career as effectively if I moved to Milwaukee. But if I *could* move to Milwaukee and earn the same salary, my living standards would soar thanks to much cheaper houses and generally lower prices of everything from food to child care.

A well-designed relocation scheme should ultimately serve the interests of federal employees as well as destination cities. But it has to be undertaken in a sane way, with plenty of notice and a phased transition.

Ideally, you'd also put a little more thought into the destinations than I did when I pulled Youngstown out of a hat as a potential home for the Bureau of Printing and Engraving. The goal should be to seek meaningful complementarities between the expertise of an agency's staff and the kind of industries present in a city. Cleveland seems like an ideal home for the National Institutes of Health and other agencies related to medical research because, as the home of the Cleveland Clinic, it already has a strength in health research.

By the same token, Detroit's enormous legacy as a center of manufacturing and engineering could make it a good home for agencies like the National Institute of Standards and Technology and relevant parts of the Patent and Trademark Office.

But perfect matching is not required. The key point is to identify cities that, like Detroit and Cleveland, are currently overbuilt from the standpoint of housing stock and infrastructure—cheap rents, few traffic jams, airports that are operating below their historical capacity—and provide them with the biggest thing they need to succeed: an infusion of new jobs and people.

Decisions of this scale are never going to be undertaken on a purely technocratic basis, but the BRAC process that shifted Defense jobs out of Crystal City is a good model for bringing technical analysis to bear on this sort of question. The government has long understood that location decisions for military facilities are in part a regional economic development policy, and there's nothing wrong with bringing the same insight to bear on civilian agencies. Then once you accept this principle, you will see there is so much further we can take it.

## Deconcentrating the private sector

I've worked now for three different media companies, each of which maintains one big office in Manhattan and another big office in Washington, DC. At each company I've often wondered if we wouldn't be better off splitting the difference and just having a single office in Philadelphia. Yes, people would need to take the train sometimes to DC or New York to report. But honestly, most of the staff at these publications are not reporting live from the Capitol or the stock exchange on a daily basis.

The cost of some extra train fare would be small compared with the savings on office space. And you could save a fair amount on train fare itself by not requiring that executives go back and forth.

In general, the extent to which not-so-lucrative fields like journalism and book publishing remain concentrated in a hyperexpensive market where companies and workers compete with hedge funds for office space and housing is remarkable. But industry clusters are remarkably resilient. A rich ecology comprising advertising agencies, ad salespeople, periodicals, writers of all kinds, book publishers, and literary agents blossoms in the shadow of Wall Street. As urban economist Ed Glaeser observes, the reason for this, historically, is that "the big money in nineteenth century books came from being the first printer out with pirated copies of English novels."*

When the Erie Canal decisively made New York rather than Philadelphia the top port on the Eastern Seaboard, New York book publishers gained a decisive leg up on their Philadelphia colleagues. The rest is history.

That's a fun story about economic history, path dependency, and how markets work. But it's fundamentally not a very good reason for the twenty-first-century media industry to be concentrated in New York rather than in a much more affordable nearby large city that offers similar urban lifestyle amenities at much lower cost. With about 1.6 million residents, down from a historic peak of more than 2 million, Philadelphia has plenty of room for more people. And in New York, with its sky-high prices for both houses and office space, anything vacated would be quickly occupied by someone else.

The switching costs, however, are just too high. Any one media company that uprooted itself from New York and DC in favor of

---

*Edward Glaeser, *Triumph of the City: How Our Greatest Invention Makes Us Richer, Smarter, Greener, Healthier, and Happier* (New York: Penguin Press, 2011), 4.

Philadelphia would be cutting itself off from the rich talent pipelines in journalism's two main cities. And any journalists who move to Philadelphia are cutting themselves off from the diverse employer ecosystem that exists in New York and DC.

A coordinated move of many media establishments, however, could be broadly beneficial. And while the government isn't going to start deporting journalists to Philadelphia (or so we hope), helping to provide coordination and overcome collective action problems is the sort of thing governments are good for. That would start with some kind of official legislation declaring that spreading private sector jobs and opportunity out of the most expensive metro areas is a goal of national policy. You'd want to create an agency to facilitate that kind of work, with a mandate to consult with business, nonprofit, and state and local government actors. And you'd need antitrust regulators to clarify that while businesses in the same sector meeting to coordinate prices would be an illegal cartel, meeting to coordinate relocation concepts is encouraged.

At the end of the day, media and publishing on their own just aren't that big a deal economically, but a basically parallel situation exists in Silicon Valley, which is a huge deal.

The global information technology industry is concentrated in a series of office parks not quite close enough to San Francisco to qualify as suburbs because once upon a time that region was the center of transistor manufacturing. Over the decades, Silicon Valley has been a fount of innovation and wealth creation. But it's also become hellishly expensive. And the fundamentally suburban-style town layouts don't suit the sensibilities of modern young technology workers, many of whom now make inconvenient commutes from the urban centers of San Francisco and Oakland. Smaller technology companies, for this reason, have tended to set up shop downtown in San Francisco. But San Francisco itself is incredibly expensive, and the city has placed sharp curbs on the expansion of office space in part to try to keep the housing market under control.

"Tech buses" that take workers from residential parts of the city to Silicon Valley office parks have become flashpoints for social conflict; homelessness is rising amid the thriving regional economy; and conflicts around gentrification have become endemic.

Some of this can and should be solved by simply building more homes and more transportation infrastructure. But what's particularly maddening about the Bay Area's conflicts over big tech's relentless expansion is that so many American cities would benefit enormously from the arrival of thousands of well-paid office workers. In America's underpopulated cities, the expansion of the tax base alone would be a game changer. The new residents would create secondary jobs by demanding local services and construction work, ensuring that incomes would rise broadly and social problems like homelessness would go down.

But as we saw with the search for HQ2, as annoyed as tech executives may become with the local politics in the Bay Area, it fundamentally makes business sense for tech companies to have their main offices in established technology hubs.

On the other hand, moving more high-end jobs out of those hubs would make more sense for the United States of America. And as with media and publishing, if you could get several different large technology companies to move jobs in tandem, the benefits of a technology cluster could be retained.

While the government can't actually *make* a bunch of big technology companies move a bunch of jobs to midwestern cities, it's clear to everyone that the tech world's moment as the golden boy of American politics has passed. Every month now some politician or other has new complaints about Big Tech and its influence on our society and economy. The tech world, meanwhile, is increasingly angry about its treatment at the hands of politicians.

A relocation scheme doesn't resolve all of these tensions, but it should ameliorate them. Being home to Apple, Amazon, Facebook, Google, Microsoft, and Netflix, among others, is a huge achievement for the American economy. But an extremely large number of Americans don't directly experience any benefits from these companies. And that's largely because their geographical base is so narrow, and the places where they are based are suffering from such acute housing shortages that they are experienced locally as a decidedly mixed blessing.

Shifting big tech out of the Bay Area could be particularly valuable because one of the region's biggest economic assets, its unique culture of venture capital firms, is basically useless to large established players. Shifting big players out would give start-ups and smaller firms more room to expand while simultaneously seeding new cities with the stockpiles of skilled workers and rich technology executives who could launch future start-up clusters.

The guiding principle should be to learn the lesson of HQ2—major corporate location decisions are never apolitical, but America's current approach leads inevitably to a race to the bottom for subsidies and a marked tendency for new jobs to cluster in the places that least need them. The federal government ought to lean against these trends, adopting rules that curtail local subsidies, identifying national target priority areas for relocation, and authorizing tax abatement for moves only to the target cities. As discussed previously, federal regulators should encourage rather than discourage interfirm coordination about location decisions—again, if and only if the goal is to shift toward target cities—and actively seek input on what kind of federal investments could make socially beneficial location decisions possible.

There's no good way to "bring back" lost manufacturing jobs. But we've now run a decades-long experiment on the proposition that if we just leave things alone, everything will be OK. But it hasn't worked.

Adopting an agenda of one billion Americans makes it more pressing to stop letting perfectly good cities waste away due to the vicissitudes of the market, but it also creates unique opportunities to revive them with the power of more people.

## National renewal visas

Realistically, only a handful of declining cities were ever large enough to be candidates for something like a big push to relocate technology companies or federal agencies. But the landscape of the country is full of smaller cities that are operating below their historical peak population, typically with abundant housing and adequate infrastructure but questionable prospects for the future.

To an extent, these issues could be addressed with miniversions of ideas we've already discussed; for example, the state government of Massachusetts could move to Worcester from Boston and probably leave the whole state better off.

But there are just too many places that broadly fit this description—Buffalo, Binghamton, Utica, Rome, Syracuse, and Rochester in New York State alone—for big centralized efforts to do all the work. These are the kinds of places that would benefit from both broader national population growth and a targeted idea that's gaining more mainstream support.

Adam Ozimek of Moody's Analytics along with John Lettieri and Kenan Fikri, from the Economic Innovation Group, call it Heartland Visas,* and the idea has been embraced, under slightly different names, by a bipartisan resolution passed by the United States Conference of Mayors.†

The key insight is that for all the troubles a city like Toledo (or Utica or Hartford or Grand Rapids) might be experiencing in global terms, Toledo is one of the very best places in the whole world to live. The weather isn't so warm but plenty of cold cities are doing fine. And while the city's median household income of $36,000 is on the low side for the United States, it compares favorably to what you'd

---

*Adam Ozimek, Kenan Fikri, and John Lettieri, "From Managing Decline to Building the Future," Economic Innovation Group, April 2019.

†John Lettieri, "Want to Fix the United States' Immigration and Economic Challenges? Try Place-based Visas," *Washington Post*, November 1, 2019, www.washingtonpost.com/opinions/2019/11/01/want-fix-united-states-immigration-economic-challenges-try-place-based-visas.

find in Poland, Hungary, Greece, Croatia, or Chile—to say nothing of India, Bangladesh, or Vietnam.

Lots of people, in other words, might jump at the chance to move to Toledo if they were given the opportunity. And we know from the lottery for H1-B visas that American companies would like to import many more foreign-born workers with technical skills than they are currently allowed to hire.

Instead of giving work permits to skilled workers that tie them to a specific company, as the United States does now, a new category of visas would tie them to a specific place.

A certain number of place-based visas would be allocated to a city—Toledo, say—that wants to opt in to the program. And then foreigners with skills who want to take a chance on Toledo can apply for a Toledo visa. If you live in the specified city for a certain period of time—five years would probably be prudent—you can convert to a regular green card. The lure of the permanent green card, among other things, is supposed to create a strong incentive to comply with the terms of the program.

In its initial form, workers who immigrate with such visas—I like to call them National Renewal Visas—would probably appeal to two partially overlapping classes of employers: information technology (IT) outsourcing companies, and companies that want to bring over more H1-B workers than they can get visas for.

As it stands, IT outsourcing companies are one of the biggest users of H1-B visas. By looking at lottery results, Michael Clemens was able to very precisely document the fact that Indian software workers earn sixfold wages when their employers are able to bring them over to the United States versus when they need to work remotely from India.* It's likely, of course, that with geographic restrictions in place, the sixfold pay increase would be reduced. But even at a mere tripling or quadrupling of wages and productivity, it would be well worth someone's while to set up a Binghamton branch office and well worth many peoples' while to move and work there for a few years.

Many recipients of National Renewal Visas will just move on after their five years are up. If they choose to do so, that's fine—even their presence as temporary workers will help bolster local economies in need. But inevitably some will end up putting down roots over the course of their five-year term and stay longer—perhaps raising families and staying permanently. And once a few immigrants choose to stay, they'll form the core of a new ethnic community that serves to attract residents. And those incremental residents will have all the usual benefits we've rehearsed over and over again— a stronger local tax base, more demand for local services, property values high enough to build wealth and support a local construction industry, as well as higher productivity for native workers.

Beyond the obvious case of tech workers, National Renewal Visas could be used to recruit medical professionals, teachers, accountants, and other skilled professionals giving businesses based in cities that opt in to the program a leg up. And over time, some visa recipients would launch their own businesses. Most likely these would mostly

---

*Michael A. Clemens, "The Effect of International Migration on Productivity: Evidence from Randomized Allocation of U.S. Visas to Software Workers at an Indian Firm," Center for Global Development, December 3, 2012, www.aeaweb.org/conference/2013/retrieve.php?pdfid=459.

be modest undertakings, but at least a few of them could turn into high-growth start-ups that would naturally be attractors for both native-born workers and immigrants.

Feel-good stories of immigrants helping to revitalize cities that have fallen on hard times are already journalistic clichés—in part because they're really true. Depressed cities gain enormously from new residents, and immigrants benefit enormously from the opportunity to live in the United States. But we should also be honest. As valuable as the contributions made by refugees in places like Lancaster, Pennsylvania, and Lewiston, Maine, have been, these are not immigrants who've been selected because of the contributions they can make. National Renewal Visas would build on those success stories, but also specifically seek out immigrants with professional skills who are likely to provide maximum value to the surrounding community. And these communities, once stabilized and growing, will be ideal places, thanks to their greater affordability, for young families to raise children and prosper.

## New universities

An agenda to spread prosperity more evenly across the country should take seriously the idea of creating new institutions—especially new institutions of higher education.

Progressive America is currently very activated around the problem of high college tuition and excessive student debt. But when you look under the hood, the current movement for free college looks more like a slogan than a real program for action. The key is that while politicians want to offer free public college degrees, the federal government doesn't actually run public colleges and universities. What's actually being proposed is not that the federal government make college free, but that it establish a grant program to partially cover the cost of eliminating tuition for states that want to opt in. That's an OK idea. But interested members of the public should be aware that in most cases, state governments are likely to turn down this offer. To the extent that states do opt in, the fiscal consequences are a bit perverse because the match structure essentially means that previously stingier states will get more money than states that did more to constrain tuition growth.

The match structure also in practice means that more money will flow to the relatively well-funded elite flagship universities that charge higher tuition than to more modestly funded institutions.

Last but by no means least, not nearly enough attention has been paid to the reality that public university presidents seem to have little interest in this idea.* In part that's because veterans of state legislative fights over funding know how unlikely it is that matching programs built around eliminating tuition will actually be appealing to state legislators. But in part it's because of a reasonable fear that accepting a short-term infusion of funds in exchange for permanently abjuring tuition will mean smaller budgets over the long term.

---

*Catherine Rampell, "Free College for Everyone? School Presidents Aren't Impressed," *Washington Post*, December 23, 2019, www.washingtonpost.com/opinions/free-college-for-every one-school-presidents-arent-impressed/2019/12/23/ad11765e-25c9-11ea-9c21-2c2a4d2c 2166_story.html.

Meanwhile, beyond tuition and debt levels, the proposal to simply subsidize more leaves unaddressed all kinds of questions around completion rates (the most serious student debt issues are among dropouts rather than graduates) and quality.

The goal of free tuition makes sense to me despite these problems. But in the existing university system it's one that fundamentally has to be pursued through state legislatures, which are the ultimate decision makers anyway.

An underrated way for the federal government to contribute—one that could also promote regional economic development—is by actually creating new universities. The federal government already offers free college via the military service academies, and the system works well. That's a model that could easily be extended to other forms of public service, with new federally funded academies dedicated to training people for careers in law enforcement and diplomacy or to work as public school teachers. Beyond these fairly specialized careers, both George Washington and Ulysses S. Grant advocated for the creation of something like a civil service academy that could teach the wide range of hard science and social science topics for which both federal and state governments require experts.

In principle, of course, new national universities could go anywhere. But it would be best to partner them with underpopulated cities that are prepared to provide the land (and in some cases actual buildings), and then reap the benefits of an influx of students, jobs, and—in some ways most important—research.

The research function of universities tends to get left out of the free college conversation. But it's critically important both for advancing human knowledge in general and also as a boost to local economies. Indeed, two economists with the New York Fed, Jaison Abel and Richard Deitz, have found that university research spending does more to create a well-educated surrounding city than does increasing the number of students taught.* This is slightly counterintuitive, but the basic issue is that students often move elsewhere after graduation. Research, by contrast, not only directly pulls in skilled workers to do the research but also creates "spillovers" into the private sector that build a more advanced local economy.

MIT economists Jonathan Gruber and Simon Johnson, in their book *Jump-Starting America*, advocate spending $100 billion a year to create new research parks located in depressed areas. That's a lot of money, but the evidence is overwhelming that money spent on basic research is a good idea. And locating new research spending in places that have housing to spare and a desperate need for more good-paying jobs is a no-brainer.

But as Bloomberg columnist Noah Smith points out, most research shows that research parks underperform traditional universities in terms of sparking innovation perhaps because universities "have systems in place for facilitating tacit exchange of knowledge through seminars, networking events and casual social interactions among researchers."†

The smart strategy would be to take Gruber and Johnson's

---

*Jaison Abel and Richard Deitz, "Do Colleges and Universities Increase Their Region's Human Capital," *Journal of Economic Geography* 12, no. 3 (May 2012): 667–91, https://doi.org/10.1093 /jeg/lbr020.

†Noah Smith, "How to Spread Tech Across America," *Bloomberg,* December 18, 2019, www .bloomberg.com/opinion/articles/2019-12-18/how-to-spread-tech-across-america.

ambition and funding goals but primarily channel the money through existing institutions of higher education. But instead of giving the money to the elite institutions that already have the easiest time attracting philanthropy, use it to build up second-tier institutions in struggling places into real research powerhouses. Creating a brand-new university or two in places like Appalachia or the Mississippi Delta, which don't have many, wouldn't be a terrible idea either.

The point across all these themes is that with a moderate amount of targeting—targeting of federal employment, targeting of private sector expansion, targeting of university funding, and even targeting of immigration—a politics of growth can and should be first and foremost a politics of regional convergence and national renewal. The so-called rust belt is packed with potential, and its cities enjoy some of the highest quality of life ever achieved anywhere on the globe. They are nonetheless struggling with the difficult challenge of population loss, but with a modicum of determination and a desire to embrace growth, these problems can be easily fixed.

But, of course, a much-larger America also requires us to find ways to get more people into the cities that are already straining.

# PART III

# We Can Have Nice Things

## CHAPTER 7

# Curing Housing Scarcity

While many American cities and increasingly their suburbs are clearly underpopulated, there is another set of metropolitan areas, mostly on the coasts, that are struggling with endemic housing affordability problems.

The scarce supply of housing in these cities is itself a cause of slow population growth because it greatly raises the costs (in either money or commuting time) of having additional children. This is particularly notable because as expensive as housing is generally in America's big coastal metropolitan areas, the cost issues in places with access to the precious "good schools" are particularly severe.

Drastically increasing the country's population threatens to make these affordability issues worse even if we take action to decentralize economic activity away from the coasts.

The good news is that policy solutions to housing scarcity are easily at hand. Much of America has tied itself in knots for years over an inability to build enough housing for people to live in, but this is not because of any technical or financial barriers to doing it—it's a simple question of changing the rules to allow more construction where there is demand for it.

## Using the best technology

Some problems are hard to solve because we literally do not know how to solve them. There is currently no reliable treatment for methamphetamine addiction. There's no cure for cancer and no vaccine for the common cold. Someday, one hopes, these problems will be solved as, over the centuries, so many technical problems have been.

Once upon a time, the question of how to safely and conveniently house a large number of people on a fixed plot or on in-demand land was an unsolved technical problem. At a certain height, buildings were prone to falling down. And after two or three flights of stairs, additional verticality becomes highly undesirable as a basic lifestyle issue. If more people wanted to live in a given place, you'd quickly reach a point where they just couldn't—even though the transportation technology that prevailed before the automobile created very strong incentives to live in a desirable location.

Today very little of this is true.

Modern building materials are not unlimited in their potential verticality, but it is possible to build vast towers out of steel and concrete. Modern mass timber structures can be built cheaply and safely for structures up to eighteen stories high, and additional progress is continually being made on this front.* Thanks to elevators, there's nothing inconvenient about living on a high floor—indeed, you get nice views and it's generally quieter and more desirable.

Obviously, not everybody wants to live in a tall apartment building (nor should they have to). By the same token, many people don't like to fly on airplanes. But whether you enjoy flying or not, the fact is that thanks to modern technology, it's always *possible* to get to Chicago pretty quickly from basically any American city. Some people can't easily afford the airfare, of course. But America is on the whole an affluent society, and most middle-class people could buy a ticket.

By the same token, modern technology ought to make it broadly possible for a middle-class person to afford a decent-sized home in any city in America. But it doesn't. Even though the technology exists to make housing abundant wherever it is in demand, the technology is not used very widely. Indeed, across the bulk of America's land area, it's illegal. The restriction is the same as if only a handful of big planes were allowed to fly into Chicago, leaving the rest of the slots for small regional jets and thus creating systemic shortages and high prices.

Air travel—like housing—is a complicated subject. But one aspect of it is very simple: If you severely curtailed the use of the best technology available for getting people to Chicago, it would be a lot

*Antonio Pacheco, "International Code Council Moves to Embrace Taller Mass Timber Buildings," *Architect's Newspaper*, January 11, 2019, https://archpaper.com/2019/01/international-code-council-taller-mass-timber-buildings.

harder to get to Chicago. And that's what America has done with its land use policy across big swaths of both coasts and increasing numbers of other communities too.

# The geography of housing scarcity

Housing scarcity is at its most acute in the San Francisco Bay Area where the rapid growth of Silicon Valley companies, the geography of the bay, and antidevelopment politics have intersected to create a disaster.

It's typical for "affordability" metrics to look at something like the ratio of housing costs to incomes, but this actually winds up understating the problem. The Bay Area is unusually rich, both because of abundant economic opportunity and because of the tight housing market pushing working-class people away. But to say that a region becomes more affordable when it drives away its poorest resident, thus raising median incomes, is perverse. The better metric to look at is the same one we used when discussing depressed cities— the ratio of the cost of a typical house to the cost of replacing the typical house if it was destroyed.

In the San Jose/Sunnyvale/Santa Clara market that includes Silicon Valley, the ratio is more than 3.5, while in the San Francisco area it's nearly 3. No place else is quite so bad, but throughout California and the Northeast, city after city has houses that cost much less to buy than they would cost to replace if they blew away. Seattle, Portland, and Honolulu are also expensive, making it tempting to shorthand this as a problem facing coastal cities. But Denver is also getting up there. And so is Austin. If you delve into the data, you'll see that a number of smaller college towns—including places like Madison, Wisconsin, that are in otherwise very affordable regions—are also getting awfully pricey.

This is in part a problem of "affordable housing," as the term is normally used in policy debates. All over the country there are people who cannot afford a decent place for their families to live. But in the most expensive markets, there are more such people. And a shocking fact about the broken state of American housing policy is that not only are there hundreds of thousands of people experiencing homelessness on any given night, the problem was getting worse even in the two years before COVID-19 hit, when the unemployment rate was falling. Indeed, the problem tends to be most severe in cities like Seattle that are experiencing economic booms.

To an extent, poor people struggle with housing problems simply because they are poor, and giving them more money—or rent subsidies—is the straightforward way to ameliorate the problem. The Supplemental Nutrition Assistance Program (SNAP) operates so that everyone who meets the income eligibility criteria is guaranteed to get benefits. Housing assistance in the United States isn't like this, and about three-quarters of the families who meet the criteria don't actually get help. That ought to change.

But there is a second difference. When the broader economy improves, food insecurity declines and the need for SNAP falls. That's because America's market for groceries fundamentally works pretty well—poor people just need some help accessing it. But as the broad economy improves, housing insecurity gets worse—a clear indication that something more fundamental has gone wrong.

## The return of land scarcity

It's no mystery why a house might cost more to buy than to build—it's because houses usually come with land attached and land can be expensive. Given the right setting, even a broken-down shack can sell for huge sums of money. A few years back, an eighty-year-old, nine-hundred-square-foot house in Palo Alto sold for more than $2.5 million and became the poster child for how land scarcity drives the housing crisis.[*]

At the dawn of the economics profession, land scarcity loomed extremely large as a consideration.

To the nineteenth-century British economist David Ricardo, diminishing returns were the central fact of economics. He felt that as a country's population grows, people would increasingly need to move not to places where incomes were highest but to places where land was cheapest. That cheap land would be lower quality than the already occupied land, either because of its intrinsic agricultural prospects or because of its access to markets. So newer farmers would end up earning lower wages—having either lower incomes or needing to toil for longer—than the established ones. Con-

---

*Brock Keeling, "Palo Alto Teardown Sells for $623K Over Asking," *Curbed*, April 26, 2017, https://sf.curbed.com/2017/4/26/15439048/silicon-valley-teardown-sold-home-house.

sequently, over time as population grows, a country's average income falls.

Capital investments can help to a degree. You can use irrigation to make land more fertile, or build canals to improve market access. But the most cost-effective improvements would be made first, and diminishing returns would set in again. What's more, improvements would serve to further increase the price of land. In the long term, all the rewards to hard work and investment would ultimately manifest themselves in rents earned by landlords—hence the dismal science.

The Industrial Revolution changed all that by dramatically reducing the economic significance of agriculture.

But the transition to a service-oriented economy has brought land scarcity back with a vengeance. Thanks to trucks, railroads, and shipping containers, an economically useful factory can be in all kinds of places. But a teacher, a dental hygienist, a cook, a surgeon, or a nanny has to live within a reasonable distance of her customers.

Fortunately, for the vast majority of modern Americans who have cars, the solution castigated as "sprawl" by its opponents works perfectly well. A working-class family living in the Oklahoma City metro area may not be able to afford a house in the absolute best school district or nicest neighborhood, but through the logic of "drive until you qualify," it can get a house somewhere. The expansive urban footprints that result aren't always very aesthetically charming, and hyperdependence on automobiles raises public health and ecological problems. But "build more highways and make the city bigger" does pretty much work as a solution to the problem of land scarcity.

But coastal cities, cities surrounded by mountains, or cities (like many on the West Coast) that are both have less land in which to sprawl. And Northeast corridor cities are close enough together that in many directions the sprawl from one city runs into another, and there's nowhere else to grow. Even cities like Houston and Atlanta with sprawl-friendly topography face the problem that as they grow, the logistics of getting around them even with a car and plenty of highway funding get worse and worse and worse. In all these cases, land scarcity bites.

The good news is that many solutions are available.

## We need all kinds of homes

The most typical dwelling in the United States is what's known to housing nerds as the "single-family detached house." Normal people just call it a house.

That's a structure—whether large or modestly sized—that's intended to be one home and which is surrounded on all sides by open space. The detached single-family home has a lot of advantages, including privacy and quiet plus plenty of outdoor space for grilling or for kids or a dog to play. It's also basically guaranteed that a block full of detached single-family houses will have plenty of places for people to park. America is full of houses like this largely because people like them and because Americans are prosperous enough to get most of what they want from their dwellings.

But this style of housing does have some significant drawbacks.

Most relevant to our concerns, they consume a very large amount of land per family. A duplex, where two families share a lot and where the two dwellings share a common wall, is both less land intensive and moderately cheaper to build (fewer walls). Town houses, where you build a bunch of single-family homes, each one sharing a wall with its neighbors, are more efficient still. On my block, and most of the blocks in my neighborhood, row houses are the most common dwelling types, with three stories above a semibasement. It's typical to divide the structure into either two separate two-story homes or else (like mine) a three-story main house that rests above a small separate apartment that occupies the basement.

An even more economical use of land is to build a big proper apartment or condo building. Really tall towers require you to use more expensive construction methods, but this can still be cost effective in the places with the very most expensive land.

But modestly sized apartments, typically built these days out of engineered wood products rather than steel and concrete, are basically the cheapest thing you can build per square foot of dwelling. The ability to safely construct multifamily apartments out of wood frames is a relatively new development in the United States, but because the process is cheap, these stick buildings have been proliferating in recent years.

If you've noticed an annoying trend toward uniform-looking new construction—"blocky mid-rises" that "range from three to seven stories tall and can stretch for blocks," as Justin Fox put it in his feature on the trend for *Businessweek*—then you're not alone. These buildings really are on the uninspired side. But they get the job done in terms of giving people places to live. And consequently, Fox writes, "They really are everywhere . . . and they're going up fast."[*]

But they're not actually *everywhere*.

In fact, they're mostly illegal! The vast majority of America's developed land is zoned exclusively for single-family detached homes. That's true not just in suburbs, but in central cities. Three-quarters of the residential land in Seattle, for example, is set aside for single-family detached houses.[†] That means you can't build duplexes—to say nothing of seven-story wood-frame apartments—throughout the majority of the central city, much less the broader metropolitan area. An older East Coast city like DC is a bit more flexible, allowing row houses and duplexes across big swaths of the city, but it still bans apartments from 75 percent of its taxable land mass.[‡] Even in New York City, fully 15 percent of residential land is set aside for the exclusive use of single-family detached houses.[§]

Obviously if you make it illegal to deploy the best available technology for conquering land scarcity, then land scarcity will become a serious problem. And, indeed, Joseph Gyourko, Jonathan Hartley,

---

[*]Justin Fox, "Why America's New Apartment Buildings All Look the Same," *Bloomberg Businessweek*, February 13, 2019, www.bloomberg.com/news/features/2019-02-13/why-america-s-new-apartment-buildings-all-look-the-same.

[†]Mike Rosenberg, "Seattle's Housing Crunch Could Be Eased by Changes to Single-family Zoning, City Report Says," *Seattle Times*, December 3, 2018, www.seattletimes.com/business/real-estate/city-report-widespread-single-family-zoning-is-damaging-seattle-and-needs-changing.

[‡]Yesim Sayin Taylor, "Single-family Zoning and Neighborhood Characteristics in the District of Columbia," D.C. Policy Center, July 17, 2019, www.dcpolicycenter.org/publications/single-family-zoning-2019.

[§]Alec Schierenbeck, "End Single-family Zoning in New York City," *Daily News*, September 18, 2019, www.nydailynews.com/opinion/ny-oped-end-single-family-zoning-in-new-york-city-20190918-hjg6oh6c5vbzxon4mjjimr2eky-story.html.

and Jacob Krimmel developed a new national index of land use regulation for the Wharton School and found that "regulation in most large coastal markets increased over time," leading inevitably to more and more housing scarcity in key places.[*]

Unfortunately, debates over the wisdom (or lack thereof) of this kind of policy tend to degenerate into a kind of toxic identity politics rather than a discussion of what we're trying to accomplish as a country.

## Good things shouldn't be required

In classic big picture ideological terms, economic regulation is what people on the left do and people on the right warn that overregulation will create big problems for society.

That is essentially what has happened with land use policy in the United States, and the problem is most severe in politically progressive jurisdictions. Politically conservative portions of the United States tend to be poorer, but in large part thanks to laxer land use rules and cheaper housing are able to offer what is in many cases a higher standard of living for many people.

But in recent years, a reform movement has taken root. This movement has ended exclusive single-family zoning in the City of Minneapolis and across most of the State of Oregon, while largely

---

[*]Joseph Gyourko, Jonathan Hartley, and Jacob Krimmel, "The Local Residential Land Use Regulatory Environment Across U.S. Housing Markets: Evidence from a New Wharton Index," National Bureau of Economic Research, December 2019, www.nber.org/papers/w26573.

eliminating it in California under the guise of allowing homeowners to add accessory dwelling units to their properties. A key rhetorical strategy of reformers has been to take advantage of progressives' increased attention to racial justice issues in recent years by noting the largely racist origins of single-family zoning as a concept. This has proved to be a fairly effective political tactic in a number of deep-blue jurisdictions. But when recently elected Virginia state legislator Ibraheem Samirah introduced legislation to legalize duplexes throughout Virginia, it prompted a nascent backlash from some conservatives.

Even as Emily Hamilton, an urban policy expert at the free market Mercatus Center, hailed Samirah's proposal as "a fairer way to allow more housing to be built," Luke Rosiak of the conservative *Daily Caller* was leading the charge of opposition. The Fairfax County Republican Party picked up his piece under the banner "Dems Declare War on Suburbs" and then while debating the piece on Twitter, Rosiak castigated "urban (central) planner soy boys" who "have never left their fancy white neighborhoods in DC to realize how much of outer suburbs are filled with people who value nature+rugged individuality & live on acreage."*

If the move to reform land use policy in the United States is understood as an attack on "the suburbs" or on the concept of living in a single-family home, then the reform cause is bound to lose. Most people live in the suburbs; most people live in single-family homes;

---

*Kriston Capps, "With New Democratic Majority, Virginia Sees a Push for Denser Housing," *CityLab*, December 20, 2019, www.citylab.com/equity/2019/12/virginia-legislature-statewide-upzoning-law-codes-ordinance/602818.

and most people are going to continue to do so under any conceivable policy paradigm.

But by the same token, while most people prefer to drive a car equipped with automatic transmission, you are certainly *allowed* to drive with standard transmission or to eschew car ownership altogether. And while in certain parts of the country it's typical for people to drive trucks for a mix of practical and cultural reasons, you're *allowed* to drive a compact sedan—or even a Prius—whether you live in Los Angeles or rural Texas. Some people own toaster ovens; other people own old-school toasters for slices; some people own both; and others own neither. It's the beauty of American freedom. And the fact that there is no regulatory requirement to equip your kitchen with a toaster is not a "war on toast," a negative judgment against people who like toasters, or an effort to say that toast, toasters, or people who love them are bad.

It's simply an acknowledgment of the fact that individual situations vary, preferences differ, and sometimes people need to make trade-offs. We toast bread frequently in my house and don't have a lot of counter space, so we have a small toaster rather than a toaster oven. That makes the most sense for us, all things considered, even though in the abstract I'd really rather have a toaster oven.

The point is that just because something is desirable doesn't mean it makes sense to *require* it—a concept American policy makers have little trouble grasping in almost any context other than housing.

Detached homes with yards are nice, most people like them, and in the natural order of things lots of people will build them and own them. But most people also like convenient commutes, and most

people also have limited amounts of money. Under the circumstances, some people would naturally prefer a denser dwelling in a
more convenient location over a more-expensive or less-convenient
alternative. The United States is, on the whole, a very sparsely populated country and would continue to be sparsely populated even if
our population tripled. There is plenty of room out there for big
houses and big lawns. But it's not economically reasonable to require
them when many people might make other choices. And while most
people will probably continue living in single-family homes, if we
want to grow we are going to need to add a lot of apartments too—
especially in our most expensive cities—and the government shouldn't
stand in the way of doing that.

## Beyond zoning

One issue to note as the national conversation around single-family
zoning matures is that there is a lot more to land use than zoning
per se.

Typical American land use regulations dictate both the uses of
structures that are allowed in a given area (residential, commercial,
or mixed) and also the form that the structures themselves may
take. My house, for example, lies inside DC's RF-1 zone, for "residential flats." RF buildings may contain either one or two units, which
provides some flexibility in terms of uses. They are also allowed to
be directly adjacent to the building next door—row houses or town
houses, rather than detached dwellings.

That's a lot more density than is permitted in most American neighborhoods. But the actual shape of the buildings is still tightly constrained. Each building must, unless it's grandfathered in, have at least one off-street parking space associated with it. No more than 60 percent of the lot can be occupied by structures. And the buildings are limited to three floors plus a basement—and thirty-five feet of total height. In practice that means most buildings have a small backyard that incorporates space for one or two cars to park behind the yard, plus a tiny front yard. Many homeowners in the area might prefer to construct a small garage to store their cars, but that would be illegal because it would violate the 60 percent occupancy rule (a previous owner of my house had an illegal garage built at some point, so mine is grandfathered in). But you also can't (legally at least) do without the parking space and have a bigger yard—even in our dense neighborhood that's walkable to much of downtown and is near a Metro station. And I certainly can't convert my garage into a small apartment to rent out. Even though the city government ostensibly believes that we have an affordable housing problem and that climate change is a big deal, you're not allowed to turn parking spaces into homes.

The crucial point is that even though "upzoning" the RF-1 portion of the city to allow for triplexes and quadplexes would be a good idea, the practical impact would be limited as long as the building forms can't change.

This is one reason why something like Houston's infamous lack of zoning ends up meaning less in practice than you might think. The city still has mandatory minimum parking requirements, building setback rules, and other restrictions on how developed land may be used. These rules—and the potential to change them—make a real difference even in a sprawling, car-oriented city whose metro area is generally pretty affordable. Up until 1999, for example, the city required houses to have minimum lots of 5,000 square feet. But that year they reduced the minimum lot size within the city's innermost loop highway to just 1,400 feet—in effect legalizing town houses.

"That decision set off an explosion of 'townhouse' type developments in inner neighborhoods," according to Daniel Hertz, "adding significant amounts of housing while retaining, generally, the basic form of a single-family home."[*]

The Houston town house boom carries several important lessons. One is that there was pent-up demand for denser housing types even in a city that's synonymous with sprawl. If town houses blossom when legalized in Houston, imagine the potential for building them in the pricey suburbs of America's big coastal cities. But another lesson is that all the dimensions of land use regulation matter. Outside of Houston, most local governments in the United States use zoning codes as their primary tool for blocking new house construction. But if state legislatures decide to try to force them to accept more housing by changing zoning law, localities can always fight back by raising parking requirements, lowering permitted heights, and changing lot occupancy and lot size rules.

---

[*]Daniel Hertz, "Why Houston Has Been Special Since at Least 1999," City Observatory, June 16, 2016, http://cityobservatory.org/why-houston-has-been-special-since-at-least-1999.

In other words, you can make a town allow duplexes but if the town says a duplex is going to need ten off-street parking spaces then nobody is going to build any.

These concerns are not merely hypothetical. Way back in 2002, the California State Legislature attempted to address the state's housing crisis by allowing single-family homeowners to build "accessory dwelling units" (aka granny flats or mother-in-law apartments). But as Margaret Brinig and Nicole Stelle Garnett showed, local governments simply responded by "imposing burdensome procedural requirements that are contrary to the spirit, if not the letter, of the state-law requirement that ADUs be permitted 'as of right,' requiring multiple off-street parking spaces, and imposing substantive and procedural design requirements."[*]

It was only about fourteen years later that a new, stronger pro-housing coalition emerged in the state legislature, passed a series of new rules designed to allow ADUs, and an ADU boom began.[†] Then in 2019, the legislature responded by passing a package of five new ADU laws—four aimed at further knocking down local barriers, and one allowing homeowners to build two ADUs rather than just one—fueling a further boom.[‡]

---

[*]Margaret Brinig and Nicole Stelle Garnett, "A Room of One's Own? Accessory Dwelling Unit Reforms and Local Parochialism," *Urban Lawyer*, 2013, https://scholarship.law.nd.edu/law_faculty_scholarship/286.

[†]Josh Cohen, "California ADU Applications Skyrocket After Regulatory Reform," *Next City*, January 4, 2018, https://nextcity.org/daily/entry/california-adu-applications-skyrocket-after-regulatory-reform.

[‡]Patrick Sisson, "Will California's New ADU Laws Create a Backyard Building Boom?" *Curbed*, October 11, 2019, www.curbed.com/2019/10/11/20909545/adus-development-california-real-estate-housing-shortage.

ADUs alone aren't going to solve the California housing crunch. For starters, by law they need to be small, which limits their potential as a housing solution for families. But the initial failure followed by later success of ADU reform shows that there's no one silver bullet to unlocking construction. What it takes, fundamentally, is for state legislatures to *want* to reduce housing scarcity, at which point they can start working creatively to eliminate barriers to house building. The key is that the technical aspects of fitting more people onto scarce land are not difficult—it's a question of politics, and in particular the kinds of political entities that are empowered to make decisions.

## The neighborhood defenders

American land use policy decisions tend to be local—extremely local.

Rules are written by cities and towns rather than states or the federal government. And when decisions are made, there are strong traditions of deferring to the local elected official who represents the land in question rather than having a true citywide decision-making process. But even beyond that, in practice the approval and permitting process tends to involve an intensive array of community meetings whose approval is either de jure or de facto required in order to move forward.

This introduces two wrinkles into the process.

One is simply that the kinds of people who show up at community meetings are not even close to being representative of the community whose interests are supposedly at issue.

For their book, *Neighborhood Defenders*, Boston University political scientists Katherine Levine Einstein, David Glick, and Maxwell Palmer were able to take advantage of Massachusetts public records laws to secure a comprehensive analysis of every citizen participant at planning and zoning meetings throughout the Greater Boston metropolitan area. They find that the people who show up are "overwhelmingly opposed to new housing proposals and demographically unrepresentative of their broader communities."[*]

Comparing meeting attendees to voter registration files, they find that participatory democracy attracts a group of people who are older, whiter, richer, and more likely to be homeowners than the local electorate. This is striking because across the country the electorate itself is older, white, richer, and more likely to own a home than the population at large. And while the authors are not able to secure equally comprehensive information on land use participation elsewhere, the evidence they have suggests that this is not a Boston-specific demographic skew.

The second wrinkle, however, is more ideological. William Fischel, one of the leading legal scholars of land use, posited his "homevoter hypothesis" years ago, stipulating that in local politics the main actors would be homeowners seeking to preserve the value of their

---

*Katherine Levine Einstein, David M. Glick, and Maxwell Palmer, *Neighborhood Defenders: Participatory Politics and America's Housing Crisis* (New York: Cambridge University Press, 2019), 111.

investment.* Einstein, Glick, and Palmer find some evidence for that but also evidence that locally oriented participants impede even new projects that would pretty clearly tend to increase local property values (replacing a warehouse with new condos, for example). They are, after all, not just voters but active participants in land use politics— people who've chosen to take time out of their day to show up to public meetings and muck around in the development process.

This participation self-selects not just demographically but dispositionally and ideologically for busybodies who see themselves as protecting the integrity of the existing neighborhood from hostile outside forces.

The problem is that while the costs of this locally based opposition to new housing are high, they are diffuse and spread throughout a region, meaning that there are no good ways to overcome them on a city-by-city basis.

## Microdecisions, macroconsequences

The fundamental problem of locally based housing policy is this: no one neighborhood's decision to allow for more construction will alter a regional housing shortage. Consequently, even voters and interest groups who might want to alleviate a regional housing shortage aren't properly motivated to engage in local fights.

---

*William A. Fischel, *The Homevoter Hypothesis: How Home Values Influence Local Government Taxation, School Finance, and Land-Use Policies* (Cambridge, MA: Harvard University Press, 2005).

By contrast, a person worried that a new development will have some kind of specific negative impact on himself or his neighborhood is highly motivated to come out and complain.

This leads to fundamentally asymmetrical politics in which the upside of overall housing abundance is never on the agenda, only the downsides of a specific project.

That's why reformers have increasingly focused their efforts on state legislatures. Viewed broadly, housing shortages are a big problem in California. They're a problem for many individual citizens; they're a problem for California business; and they're a problem for California's public sector labor unions, which need a growing population to keep pension systems viable. That's why the legislature was ultimately willing to pass tough ADU reforms and is actively considering more sweeping measures to allow denser construction in transit- and job-rich corridors. Oregon's legislature, similarly, has acted to allow quadplexes across most of the state's cities—elevating the discussion to the state level brings a broader set of concerns into view and leads to different outcomes.

Based on these successes, enterprising legislators have introduced reform proposals in Virginia and Maryland, and one hopes similar ideas will spread to New Jersey, New York, Connecticut, and Massachusetts, where they are sorely needed.

The national perspective on this is also valuable. Greater housing supply would mean more opportunity for Americans to move to opportunity.

But for our purposes the most important thing is that it would allow for a much larger overall national population. For starters, the high cost of housing is itself a major barrier to having and raising children. An elevated share of twentysomethings living with their parents isn't good news for the prospects of marriage and family formation. And while many young couples in America's priciest metro areas end up deciding to move to more abundant housing in the sun belt when they start having kids, many others stick with expensive cities where cost becomes a consideration in limiting family size.

Similarly, right now places like New York and California, which attract large inflows of immigrants, tend to generate large outflows of native-born Americans. This phenomenon generates an endless stream of hot takes—*Governing* magazine asked in the winter of 2018, "Why are so many people moving out of the Northeast"* and catalogued a bunch of possibilities—but it's essentially a mechanical requirement.

A lot of people would like to live in New York City—if they didn't, it would be cheap—but if the city and its inner suburbs make it hard to build new homes, then each newcomer needs to replace someone who is leaving.

On the left this frequently manifests itself as anxiety about "gentrification," and the villains are said to be upscale white professionals. On the right, it's immigrants staging a "great replacement." In both cases, however, the real villain is bad housing policy. There's nothing wrong with a city being a desirable place to move to—that

---

*Michael Maciag, "Why Are So Many People Moving Out of the Northeast," *Governing*, December 21, 2018.

means you're doing something right—it's the sense that newcomers can't be housed in new buildings that drives all the problems.

If you believe that there's a strong national interest in making the country larger—and therefore both richer and more powerful on the national stage—then there's a strong interest in adopting federal measures to alleviate housing scarcity.

## A national growth compact

There are currently a few different bipartisan legislative proposals in Congress to encourage more house building, plus the 2020 Democratic Party primary generated several plans from presidential contenders.

It's not actually important to find and praise one specific best idea for improving federal housing policy. The essential problem here is political, and the politicians themselves are best equipped to figure out what can pass and sustain enduring coalitions. But most current proposals are flawed in at least one of two ways.

One trap, shared by Senator Todd Young's Yes In My Backyard (YIMBY) Act and Senator Cory Booker's campaign proposal, is excessive focus on Community Development Block Grants (CDBG) as levers for incentivizing change. These proposals arise out of a narrow congressional logic that says that if you want to tackle a housing issue, you need to identify a Department of Housing and Urban Development funding stream. Once you're looking at HUD money, the CDBG program does look like the best choice.

The problem here is that the CDBG program does not offer very much money, and it's specifically targeted at poor cities. The biggest gains are in driving change in rich cities and their suburbs, where CDBG won't get the job done.

A second trap, typified by Senator Elizabeth Warren's proposal, is to make a big push to link a one-time infusion of federal money to zoning reform. It would be nice if this worked. But realistically there are so many complexities to land use policy that it would be easy for jurisdictions to eliminate the most abusive practices in exchange for money and then come up with brand-new equally effective ways of stonewalling. For the "one big push" theory of change to work, the initial federal rule would have to be perfectly drafted and loophole free. Not only is that unlikely on its own terms, any sufficiently de-tailed federal agenda would naturally provoke the counterargument that it's too prescriptive and inflexible.

The best path forward is going to be pursuing multiple channels of reform across a broad front. And ideally the federal government should keep its eyes on the prize—the production of new homes in jurisdictions where the market price is high. An ideal federal policy would link a large sum of fairly flexible money to different jurisdic-tions' success or failure at meeting that goal, while remaining ag-nostic about the exact regulatory details. If more left-wing places want to build public or nonprofit housing or impose inclusionary zoning overlays, that's fine. If more right-wing places want to rely on a purely market mechanism, that's also fine. State governments, or perhaps even local ones, can decide exactly what kinds of changes need to be made. But at the end of the day, pricey places that don't see new units should face consequences.

## Gentle and not-so-gentle density

It's become common in reformist circles to start trying to rhetorically downplay the extent of needed change. This is in some ways a useful counterpoint to demagogic rhetoric from defenders of the status quo, who like to portray reformers as fanatically focused on stacking everyone into ultradense tenements or the vast towers of Hong Kong.

This is nonsense—allowing apartments everywhere doesn't mean everyone will live in an apartment or that there will in fact be apartments everywhere. Every American is allowed to buy a pickup truck. Most don't, but many do. Some parts of the country are well suited to trucks, and lots of people in those places buy them, but not everyone does. And even in places that aren't well suited to trucks, they are well suited to some people's jobs, so they buy them. Other people just want to be eccentric and own trucks for no reason—that's fine too. It's a free country, as we used to say. Nobody is going to make you sell your detached single-family house to a developer who replaces it with a tall apartment building, and across most of the country probably nobody would even want to do that.

Housing organizer Alex Baca and Brookings Institution housing economist Jenny Schuetz talk about "gentle density," which "could increase the number of homes available and bring down average housing prices in high-cost locations, while retaining the physical scale of the neighborhood."[*]

And, indeed, allowing a few small apartments to sprout in a single-family neighborhood can drastically increase the availability of affordable housing without fundamentally altering the scale or character of the built environment.

This is a good vision of what today's pricey, auto-dependent suburbs might look like in a post-reform future. Existing single-family neighborhoods will continue to be single-family neighborhoods but will be dotted with a few apartments or town house clusters here and there.

At the same time, it would be a mistake to go too far in offering reassurance. Many jurisdictions, for example, have made enormous financial investments in building rail transit. Nevertheless, the nature of trains is that even with a lot of money spent, very little land is ever going to be incredibly close to a train station. Whether or not there's actually demand for tall apartment towers near transit stations will depend on many factors. But to the extent that there is demand, it's insane to impose arbitrary quantitative limits to the construction of transit-oriented housing.

I am privileged to live in a neighborhood from which it is convenient to walk to many downtown jobs. By definition, only a very small share of the land in any given metro area is going to be close

---

*Alex Baca, Patrick McAnaney, and Jenny Schuetz, "'Gentle' Density Can Save Our Neighborhoods," Brookings Institution, December 4, 2019, www.brookings.edu/research/gentle-density-can-save-our-neighborhoods.

to downtown. My neighbors would probably prefer that if they must accept any new density, it be "gentle." But the fact is we are sitting on top of a valuable and unique commodity—downtown-adjacent land—and it should be developed however intensively voluntary transactions will allow.

A lot of "urbanist" discourse in the United States is dominated by people who have a strong aesthetic preference for the look of neighborhoods that were built before the era of widespread car ownership. This leads then to want to replace the mandatory suburbanism that currently dominates American land use with a kind of retro-urbanism that would relegalize town houses and garden apartments without necessarily leaping all the way to towers.

These "missing middle" building types should be legal. But advocates also shouldn't kid themselves. Changing zoning won't un-invent cars or re-create the economic conditions that made little brick buildings a profitable form of construction. Given the existing technology, it genuinely makes sense for the majority of developed land to be given over to the kind of suburbs that Americans know and love (or in some cases love to hate). But on the small minority of land where vacant lots sell for four or five times the price of the median American house, it makes sense to build some pretty large buildings.

This is particularly true because while apartment living has some downsides compared with a freestanding house with a yard, living in a fourteen-story apartment doesn't really have downsides compared with living in a four-story one. On the contrary, larger-scale buildings can offer amenities like gyms, concierges, and other common facilities that don't really work in small ones.

More generally, if you look at a country that has experienced rapid economic growth over the past generation—whether it's China, India, Qatar, or whoever else you care to name—it's invariably the case that the physical landscape has been transformed.

## The dead hand of the past

Beyond zoning and other formal land use restrictions, in some American cities the kudzulike growth of historic preservation rules has become a major barrier to curing housing scarcity and making progress on other fronts as well.

Here it's important to try to be precise because the concept of "historic preservation" incorporates a wide range of practices and concepts.

At one end of the spectrum is the idea that public resources should be invested in maintaining certain noteworthy buildings even when market forces would not do so. Like anything else this could be taken too far, but it fundamentally makes a lot of sense. Just as the public sector works alongside philanthropists to ensure that we have parks and museums, it should also ensure that our cities and towns have their share of beautiful old buildings.

But the common practice of historic preservation in many American cities goes well beyond that. In DC's Cleveland Park neighborhood, for example, there's an old strip mall right next to a metro station that can't be redeveloped as a mixed-use apartment building on the theory that the strip mall is so old it's historic.* This is incredibly valuable land—in a building one block away (and thus slightly farther from the Metro) a 677-square-foot apartment sells for more than $200,000. The cost to the landlord of maintaining the strip mall is commensurately enormous. If the historic preservation law involved financially compensating property owners for the burden of regulation, there's no way the city would approve the vast appropriation that would be required. But the costs of preservation are not borne just by the property owner. Hundreds of families who could otherwise enjoy conveniently located apartments are forced elsewhere. The city's property tax base is smaller than it otherwise would be, leading to higher taxes and fewer public services for those in need.

If it were just one random strip mall, that wouldn't be so bad. But the practice of mindlessly freezing in place old structures is repeated in building after building in neighborhood after neighborhood in city after city across America.

The costs of these rules are hidden, because cities don't pay compensation to the affected property owners. But imagining what it would cost if they *did* pay is a good way of getting your head around the staggering social cost of regulating in this way.

Not only are these rules uneconomical, but they generally conflict with cities' other stated goals. Most major urban centers in the United

---

*Jacob Kaplan, "They Paved Paradise and Put Up a Park and Shop," *Boundary Stones*, July 17, 2017, https://blogs.weta.org/boundarystones/2017/07/17/they-paved-paradise-and-put-park-and-shop.

States have voting bases and elected officials who believe that climate change is a big problem. There's no reasonable way to tackle that problem without replacing much of the built environment with more modern, more energy-efficient structures. But in historically designated neighborhoods this is generally impossible. At times, cities even prevent homeowners from installing modern energy-efficient windows—insisting instead on keeping old-fashioned draftier wooden ones in place.

In specific situations one can imagine a rationale for this kind of broad-brush preservation. France derives significant economic benefits from tourist visits to Paris, visits which might plausibly dry up if the historic city were steadily replaced with modern buildings. A similar logic applies to Barcelona and a number of other European cities that have deliberately cultivated tourism as a major growth engine. In the United States that might apply to New Orleans, Miami Beach, and some small towns in New England. But it's not a relevant consideration for the major supply crunch cities.

And in general, it would not make a lot of sense for the United States to stake its economic and geopolitical future on the proposition that we're going to compete with Paris and Barcelona as old-timey tourist destinations. We have a lot going for us as a country, but this is not our strong suit. If we want to remain the world's number one power, we're going to have to embrace the reality that you can't have progress without change. We can and should stay number one forever, but it's going to mean knocking down some old buildings and finding a better way to deal with traffic jams.

CHAPTER 8

# Getting Around

Transportation in the United States is already not what it could or should be.

Indeed, this is an area of life in which in many respects we have undergone a kind of regression to a lower standard of living than was enjoyed in the past. Modern cars are, from a technical standpoint, drastically superior to the automobiles of the 1960s and 1970s. They're more fuel efficient, they're safer, they have better sound systems, they have onboard navigation—they're great. But mostly what people want to do in their cars is get from Point A to Point B, and in terms of actual travel time things have gotten worse.

According to the Texas Transportation Institute's 2019 Urban Mobility Report, across 494 metropolitan areas the average car commuter spent twenty hours per year in traffic jams back in 1982. By 2017, it was up to fifty-four hours. Adjusted for inflation, back in

1982 the trucking industry lost $1.8 billion per year in extra time and fuel costs due to congestion. By 2017, that had exploded to $19.5 billion.

And cars are not unique in having gotten slower.

While Americans have spent years debating the wisdom of investing in next-generation high-speed passenger rail, for example, the actual reality is that contemporary passenger trains go slower than the ones of generations ago.

"Going from Brattleboro, Vt., to New York City on the Boston and Maine Railroad's *Washingtonian* took less than five hours in 1938," writes Tom Vanderbilt. "Today, Amtrak's *Vermonter* (the only option) takes six hours—if it's on time, which it isn't, nearly 75 percent of the time."* And the Vermont route is not exceptional. A trip from Chicago to Denver takes five hours longer than it did in 1934. Chicago to Minneapolis has gone from four and a half hours in the 1950s to more than eight hours today.

In practice, outside of a few markets the tremendous slowdown in intercity rail isn't a big deal because trains wouldn't be competitive with planes anyway. But air travel has gotten slower too. Modern passenger planes typically cruise between 480 and 510 knots, whereas a Boeing 707 would've flown at 525 knots in the 1960s.† That's mostly because airlines have figured out that flying slower is more fuel efficient, and that saving money is more important to

---

*Tom Vanderbilt, "Stop This Train!" *Slate*, May 15, 2009, slate.com/human-interest/2009/05/why-trains-run-slower-now-than-they-did-in-the-1920s.

†Andrea Romano, "Why Flying Is Slower Now Than It Was 20 Years Ago," *Travel and Leisure*, May 11, 2018, www.travelandleisure.com/travel-news/flying-slower-now-than-20-years-ago.

customers than going slightly faster. At the same time, the airport security process has become much more cumbersome, meaning that actual total travel times have regressed considerably. Rather than making progress toward supersonic travel, we've just given up on going faster.

These are not great trends no matter what we do regarding the size of the population. But it's hard to deny that tripling the country's population is going to put more strain on the transportation system. And given that the transportation system already seems to be moving backward in terms of quality, that's a very legitimate concern.

Indeed, here's Michael Anton, a former Trump administration official and one of the main ideologists of the front-loaded traffic-jams-as-an-anti-immigrant argument in a major op-ed: "So again: Why do we need more people?" he asked. "For the extra traffic congestion? More crowded classrooms? Longer emergency room and Transportation Security Administration lines?"[*]

Some of this is absurd. If you have more people, you build more classrooms and more emergency rooms. Canada has about one-tenth of America's population, but they still have twenty-six high school students per class.[†] Fewer people means fewer high schools, not less crowding. But the transportation points will ring true to many people because it's demonstrably not the case that our infrastructure

---

*Michael Anton, "Why Do We Need More People in This Country, Anyway?" *Washington Post*, June 21, 2018, www.washingtonpost.com/opinions/why-do-we-need-more-people-in-this -country-anyway/2018/06/21/4ee8b620-7565-11e8-9780-b1dd6a09b549_story.html.

†Derek Allison, "Secondary School Class Sizes and Student Performance in Canada," Fraser Institute, October 1, 2019, www.fraserinstitute.org/studies/secondary-school-class-sizes-and -student-performance-in-canada.

has been scaling in line with the growth of our population and our economy. At the same time, the idea that America needs to shrink away from growth and greatness because we can't figure out how to manage airport security lines is depressing. The country has real transportation problems, but we ought to try to fix them rather than let a cycle of learned helplessness convince us that a strategy of national decline is the only way to manage our commutes.

## Fix the damn roads!

The most basic thing the government could do to turn the transportation situation around would be to actually prioritize the upkeep of our existing infrastructure. An eye-opening report from the advocacy group Transportation for America revealed that between 2009 and 2017 the percentage of American roadways rated as being in "poor" condition rose from 14 percent to 20 percent.[*]

During this period the federal government first sent a surge in funding to state transportation departments as part of the Obama-era stimulus bill, and then repeatedly passed bailouts of the federal highway trust fund that sent states money over and above the gasoline tax revenue set aside for that purpose.

Part of the issue is that over this period we should have been spending even more money—interest rates were low, the economy was depressed, and investments in public infrastructure would have

---

[*]Transportation for America, *Repair Priorities*, May 15, 2019.

been smart. But on another level the deteriorating state of America's roads reflects doubly perverse priorities.

For starters, states split their spending between upkeep and building new roads roughly evenly. Politicians have a strong bias toward new projects that allow for fun ribbon-cutting ceremonies versus routine maintenance work that goes largely unnoticed. But in the real world, routine low-key upkeep is much more cost-effective than allowing roads to become seriously distressed and then trying to bring them back up to par.

And the big problem with the even funding split between expansion and upkeep is that every mile of new road you add to your network also needs to be maintained. A desperately poor country with few paved roads might want to invest fairly aggressively in expansion. But the fact of the matter is that automobiles have been widely used in the United States for a long time now. There's plenty of merit to the idea of some expansion of the highway network, but the most valuable and important roads have already been built—oftentimes decades ago. New expansions at the margin have their place, but they can't reasonably substitute for upholding high-quality standards for the roads that we already have—roads that generally connect the main population centers, commercial clusters, airports, and other major destinations.

A related issue is that states split their upkeep spending roughly equally between rural and metropolitan roads. But roughly 80 percent of the population lives in America's metro areas, primarily in the auto-dependent suburbs. More people rely on these roads, and it's objectively more important that they be in tip-top shape. At the same time, precisely because they get more traffic, they experience more wear and tear and have higher needs. In effect, only a quarter of capital spending is going to ensure the ongoing health of the most-used core roads, with the rest going to rural repairs and marginal expansion projects.

Some states that are spending more on expansion than repair, such as Arizona and Nevada, are in fact growing unusually rapidly. But West Virginia is spending more on expansion even though the state's population is shrinking and has in fact been fitfully declining since about 1950. Naturally the share of West Virginia roads in poor condition is rising even as the population declines. Under the circumstances it's difficult to see what additional investment in increasingly marginal roads is supposed to accomplish.

In Washington, the concept of "fix it first" as an infrastructure priority is associated with urbanists who have a dispositional dislike of highway spending. In practice, however, if you ask which states are genuinely walking the walk on fix it first, North and South Dakota lead the way along with some more urbanized states like New Jersey.

Technocratic thinking is out of style in American politics today, but the fact remains that there really are a lot of technical questions in government and not everything is about ideology, culture war posturing, or a remorseless struggle for power. That's especially true in the transportation sector, where virtually all domains of American activity are currently beset by flawed practices. The overinvestment in expansion over upkeep is one example, but there are many—starting with the basic federal funding model.

# Beyond the gas tax

For a long time, federal surface-transportation spending was tied to the federal gasoline tax. The tax raised revenue and then the revenue was kicked out to the states—mostly for road spending, with a slice of the pie carved out for mass transit.

As long as everyone was driving internal combustion engine vehicles and Congress was prepared to periodically raise the tax, this worked pretty well.

For starters, the amount of gas tax you paid was more or less a function of how much you drove and how heavy your vehicle was. So the roads were being financed largely by the people who used them most (miles traveled) and whose activities stressed them the most (heavy vehicles). Then there was a formula for kicking money back to the states that was largely driven by how much gas tax revenue each state generated. If the various stakeholders in the automotive world wanted more money for roads, they needed to pay more gas tax—and so every once in a while the tax went up.

But ever since Newt Gingrich won a majority for House Republicans back in 1994, nobody in Congress has wanted to touch the gas tax issue. The rate has stayed fixed at 18.4 cents per gallon for nearly a generation, even as inflation has eroded the real value of those 18.4 cents. At the same time, welcome advances in fuel efficiency technology mean that contemporary cars generate less tax revenue per mile driven than they did in the past. In more recent years, the advent of electric cars and hybrids has further detached gasoline consumption from the key variables of vehicle miles traveled and vehicle weight. From a strict pollution control standpoint this is, of course, all good news. And encouraging people to adopt less-polluting modes of transportation is one valid purpose of a gasoline tax.

But America's gasoline tax isn't really structured to serve as a pure pollution control measure. It's supposed to work as a user fee to ensure that those who use and stress roads the most pay the bulk of the tab. The low-emission nature of a Tesla or a Nissan Leaf is a true technological marvel, and it's appropriate for public policy to try to incentivize a rapid switch to low-emission vehicles. But from a road-funding standpoint, Tesla drivers are still out there taking up space and a Tesla Model X is nearly as hefty as a Chevy Suburban in terms of pounds of vehicle on the pavement.

Because states generally charge vehicle registration fees along with gas taxes, many states have moved to charge higher registration fees on electric vehicles (EV) to compensate for the lost gas tax revenue they represent. Indeed, according to a late 2019 *Consumer Reports* analysis "of the 26 states that currently impose EV fees, 11 charge more than the amount owners of similar gas-powered cars pay in gas taxes, and three charge more than twice the amount."[*] The same analysis found bills to impose EV fees pending in twelve more states, of which ten were considering fees higher than the average driver's gas tax bill, and seven were ratcheting up fees over time to double what a typical internal combustion engine driver pays.

---

*Jeff Plungis, "More States Hitting Electric Vehicle Owners With High Fees, a Consumer Reports Analysis Shows," *Consumer Reports*, September 11, 2019, www.consumerreports.org /hybrids-evs/more-states-hitting-electric-vehicle-owners-with-high-fees.

The federal government, meanwhile, has just seen revenue plummet and has started routinely appropriating highway funding in excess of what the highway trust fund actually takes in.

We've landed in an incredible conceptual muddle. Charging EV drivers nothing to use the roads, as the federal government and some states do, makes very little sense and is going to become completely unviable if the country makes the transition to more sustainable modes of transportation. At the same time, charging drivers higher fees to use cleaner modes of transportation is ridiculous. To the extent the government influences the choice between conventional engines and electric ones, it should be to push for faster adoption of EVs. But in a world where many cars don't burn gasoline at all, we need to drop the idea of using gasoline taxes as a kind of user fee.

That doesn't mean we should let gasoline go untaxed—it remains a major environmental hazard and should either be taxed directly or else be taxed as part of a larger carbon tax. But the price of the tax should be driven by the negative climate and public health impacts of the emissions, and the revenue should have nothing in particular to do with funding roads.

Road funding should be driven by actual user fees. Modern technology makes it possible to actually measure how much people are driving, and where, and when. Those measurements should be used as the basis for charging drivers and funding roads. That could take the form in part of a vehicle-miles-traveled (VMT) tax, but ideally a very large share of the revenue would come from charges that are specifically linked to traffic congestion. Make drivers pay for using crowded roads at crowded times.

# Charging for congestion

Economists, policy wonks, technocrats, and pundits like me have been trying to persuade the public to embrace congestion taxes for decades with little success. So I'm realistic about the odds that a brief discussion in this book will change that calculus.

But it really is worth underscoring how important it is.

Traffic jams are extremely annoying; they waste time; they cause excess pollution; and they have been getting worse over time. And unlike the vast majority of more commonly voiced objections to immigration or a family-friendly welfare state, it really is true that a larger population will mean more traffic jams. On the other hand, it would be borderline absurd for the mightiest country in human history to abdicate all its historic aspirations and accept second-class status over a fear of traffic jams. And it's particularly perverse because there is a solution at hand to the problem of traffic jams that is well understood, works perfectly well, and on net has no financial cost. Apollo program analogies are somewhat overdone, but surely citizens of the country that sent human beings on rocket ships to stroll around the moon in the name of competition with the USSR can stir themselves to borrow Sweden's approach to managing traffic rather than just throw up their hands in the face of China and India.

The way it's worked in Stockholm since 2006 is that if you want to drive into the central city, you need to pay a toll of between eleven and thirty-five Swedish kronor (about one to four US dollars, depending on the day's exchange rate). The highest tolls are at the peak rush hour times, between 7:30 and 8:30 a.m. and between 4:00 and 5:30 p.m. A little bit earlier or a little bit later, and you pay a lower toll. Midday tolls charge the low eleven-kronor rate.

Singapore, which was the first major city to implement a congestion charge, has a somewhat more complicated system. It uses cameras to record license plates that communicate with EZ-Pass-like devices that Singaporeans keep in their cars. The fees charged vary both by time of day, vehicle type, and by where exactly in the city the car is.

Today broadly similar congestion-pricing systems are in place in London, Milan, and Oslo, and after an incredible amount of back-and-forth, it looks like New York City will move in this direction too.

In all cases, the introduction of congestion fees has been extremely controversial—people don't like taxes and tend to be mildly resistant to any kind of unfamiliar policy idea—but they've ultimately stuck around even as partisan control of the government has switched.

And that's because the logic of congestion pricing is extremely compelling.

Once a year as a marketing stunt, Ben & Jerry's stages a free ice-cream cone day when they literally give away free ice-cream cones at their stores. Ice cream is delicious, but if you go to get a cone, make sure to go with friends because the stunt invariably generates extremely long lines. As a once-a-year lark with some friends, standing in line for an hour to get ice cream is fun. But for most of us an hour of time is actually worth more than the modest price of a Ben & Jerry's cone. If you're actually hungry for ice cream—as opposed to looking for an afternoon activity—paying three or four bucks is a superior option to standing around waiting for a free cone. Everyone likes free stuff, but *precisely because* everyone likes free stuff, it leads to overcrowding.

In the case of ice cream, charging money not only solves the overcrowding problem, it also lets the company turn a profit. That's good for them but less exciting for customers.

The great news about congestion tolls, however, is that not only can they prevent the superlong lines, but the money goes to the public purse, where it can be used for public purposes. Of course nobody is going to be thrilled about paying a new tax. But it's not as if paying existing taxes is so great either. To the extent that we need a funding source for our roads, it makes a lot of sense to fund them with a tax that also accomplishes something useful.

That these systems have been politically sticky everywhere they've been tried tells us something important. Many people are intuitively skeptical of the idea that charging prices can reduce traffic volumes, but it works. And one of the reasons it works is that it can operate through so many different channels. A certain number of people will just decide not to make a trip. Some others will delay or accelerate their plans to travel at lower-priced, less-congested times. Some extra people will carpool and some extra people will ride buses or trains, or bicycle. And the magic of it is that it typically doesn't require that much reduction in traffic volume to go from a deeply overcrowded roadway to a busy but basically functioning one.

Key to getting it done, however, is making sure that improved management of America's traffic is understood as a real fix to a problem that bedevils the country rather than another front in culture war politics.

## Congestion and transit

Unfortunately, congestion pricing is often framed as a revenue raiser for investment in mass transit.

This is mistaken on two grounds, one technical and one political.

The technical flaw in the argument is that in the American context, implementing the congestion price actually generates substantial improvements in transit without any need for additional funds. The political flaw is that congestion pricing is unfamiliar and controversial, and framing it as a zero-sum financial transfer from the driving majority to the transit-riding minority sets it up for failure.

Taking the technical issue first, if you get rid of traffic congestion, then city buses will run faster. Because faster buses complete their routes more swiftly, transit agencies will be able to deliver more frequent service with no increase in cost.

All else being equal, faster buses will attract more riders than slower ones. And bus lines featuring more frequent service will attract more riders than less frequent ones. Last but by no means least, raising the price of driving will, on its own, induce some people to switch to the bus—especially because the bus service is now better. With three different factors driving bus ridership higher, the transit agency's revenue is now higher and it can hire more drivers and run more buses.

For American rail transit there are sometimes hard physical constraints to carrying more people during peak times, and it is going to be important for the cities facing such constraints to make investments to address them. But American cities have frequently made investments in rail transit that combine low frequencies with low ridership volumes.

Dallas, for example, is nobody's model of a mass transit city. But over the years the city has at great expense built out a four-line light rail system with 93 miles of track, sixty-four stations, and an annual ridership of fewer than 30 million trips. The much smaller Italian city of Turin has a one-line light rail that runs for 8.3 miles across twenty-one stations and generates more than 42 million annual trips. It's perhaps not realistic for the American sun belt to generate Italian levels of riders per track mile, but would it be so crazy to hope American cities could achieve a quarter of Italian performance? A fifth? Right now Dallas is obtaining fewer than one-tenth of Turin's ridership per mile of track built.

One key difference is the underlying nature of the urban fabric. But another is simply that if you have to be traveling the route of the Turin Metro, it's an extremely convenient way to go with trains arriving every two minutes. DART (Dallas Area Rapid Transit) Light Rail headways, by contrast, are twelve to fifteen minutes at peak hours and twenty to thirty minutes off-peak. If congestion charges induced more people to ride DART, then DART could afford to run trains more frequently, which would greatly improve the quality of DART service without any incremental investment of funds.

The point here is not to rail against the idea of increased transit funding, but simply to make the point that turning the debate over congestion pricing into a debate over transit funding is unnecessary— congestion pricing is a big win for transit riders regardless of what you do with the money. But outside of New York, transit riders are not a large enough constituency to win a political argument. The money should go to whatever the voters want—better parks, lower sales taxes, more roads, more police officers—with transit advocates secure that more riders is its own reward, and will in turn build a constituency for more transit investments.

## Better, smarter transit

Debate over mass transit in the United States tends to be excessively bedeviled by two red herrings—one is the total scale of funding and the other is the specter of innovation.

Transit advocates would, of course, like to see more money spent on mass transit. I sympathize with their views on this, and it's obvious that if we are going to triple the size of the population, we are going to need some more trains. But what's genuinely striking about mass transit investment in the United States is not how little of it there is but how little transit ridership we generate for the money. Fixing that problem would not only be valuable on its own terms, it would naturally generate the needed political momentum for increasing spending. Los Angeles alone has invested billions of dollars in recent years in constructing the Los Angeles Metro Rail system, which has less than a third of the ridership of smaller mass transit systems in much smaller cities like Budapest, Milan, Busan, Montreal, or Stockholm.

Concurrently, major political stakeholders in American mass transit are relentlessly focused on the concept of innovation, with New York governor Andrew Cuomo announcing a flashy "genius" contest to improve transit. Elon Musk, when not colonizing Mars or trying to revolutionize the car industry, muses publicly about totally reworking American urban transportation.

There's something natural about this. The United States is bad at mass transit but good at innovation, so the idea that we need to apply some innovation to our transit problem has some appeal. But it's fundamentally misguided. The countries that should be trying to innovate in the transportation space are places like Japan, Korea, and France, which are currently at the world frontier of transportation quality. The United States needs to do what the Chinese spent the first twenty years of the century doing—relentlessly copying more successful models from abroad and deferring innovation until our agencies show mastery of existing technology.

Consider the basic question of boring tunnels. New York City recently constructed a three-station short version of the Second Avenue Subway at the cost of $1.7 billion per kilometer and is trying to put together the funding for a projected second phase of the project at a cost of $2.2 billion per kilometer.* This is an order of magnitude more than what continental Europe spends on urban subway tunnels. Berlin's U-55 line cost $250 million per kilometer, Paris Metro's

---

*Josh Barro, "Why New York Can't Have Nice Things," New York, May 30, 2019.

Line 14 cost $230 million per kilometer, and Copenhagen's Circle Line cost $260 million per kilometer (and less than that in purchasing power parity terms).

Alon Levy, a quirky Israeli mathematician who did a lot of the original legwork on comparative construction costs before pivoting his career to working full time on transit issues, observes that this cost gap drives a growing divide in actual infrastructure provision. Between 2005 and 2030, New York will have spent about $35 billion on subway and commuter rail projects in exchange for fifteen kilometers of new tunnel. During the same period, Paris will spend €40 billion to build 187 kilometers of new tunnel plus about 40 more kilometers of track above ground. Madrid, the world leader in cost-effective tunneling, got 234 kilometers built (of which 180 are underground) for about €10 billion between 1995 and 2015.[*]

America could afford to spend more on mass transit projects. But by the same token, we could afford to build way more mass transit if we could get costs down to French levels. And in fact if we were getting much more tunnel per dollar spent, appropriating even more money would probably feel like a more politically compelling issue.

The cost gap is so enormous that it naturally raises the question of why. Nobody really knows for sure (fortunately, thanks largely to Levy's tireless work, a few philanthropists are now actually funding efforts to study the factors), but it's clear from initial surveys that there isn't just one single reason. Compared with the top performing

---

[*]Alon Levy, "Why Costs Matter," *Pedestrian Observations*, January 1, 2016. See also Alon Levy, "Assume Nordic Costs," *Pedestrian Observations*, May 29, 2019.

countries, the United States seems to use labor inefficiently because of union work rules but also to deliberately choose more expensive construction methods and to opt for more elaborate station design choices that dramatically increase costs with little transportation benefit. In Spain they try to break contracts down into small pieces to maximize the number of bidders, and invest heavily in developing in-house expertise to evaluate the technical merit of different proposals. US agencies do less in-house, and put out huge contracts for bids, allowing a handful of firms to dominate the process and pad their bills.

But on a higher level, the problem is one of political inattention. It shouldn't have required the work of a smart blogger to put this topic on the public agenda, but nobody at America's transportation agencies was interested enough in comparative issues to notice until outsiders began making noise. Then back in 2017 some Senate staffers got interested enough to insert a line item into legislation authorizing the federal share of financing for DC's transit agency, directing the Government Accountability Office (GAO) to do a study of comparative transit costs. But a powerful House Democrat intervened to kill that provision, fearing it might imperil a particular (and incredibly expensive) local project for which federal funding had finally been secured.* The next year, the provision was allowed to go through, but the GAO's completed report said that it was too hard to

---

*Matthew Yglesias, "Someone Killed America's Sky-high Transit Construction Costs," *Vox*, May 24, 2017, www.vox.com/policy-and-politics/2017/5/24/15681560/gao-report-transit -construction-costs.

do international comparisons and ended up mostly focusing on how American agencies could improve their cost *estimates* to avoid overruns.*

Nobody likes cost overruns, but bad estimating fundamentally does not explain why continental Europe is getting things done for a fraction of American prices. The fact that the American political system is so reluctant to look into this in a rigorous way—or to hire veterans of these cost-effective European systems to improve project management in American agencies—itself explains a fair amount of the problem.

Getting construction costs more into line with European norms would, of course, be a good idea no matter what else happens in the country. But an agenda of more rapid population growth will require more infrastructure, which makes cost-effectiveness more important. The good news is that precisely because more growth means more infrastructure, it should be easy enough to guarantee contractors that the goal here is not actually to "save money" by spending less on infrastructure. The goal is to spend a little more and in exchange *get a lot* more—but still with plenty of jobs for everyone. In France, they use a twelve-person crew on a tunnel-boring machine (TBM), while America uses twenty-five. We don't need to fire half the TBM operators; what we should do is hire 50 percent more but insist on building three times as many tunnels.

---

*Alon Levy, "New Report on Construction Costs Misses the Mark," *Pedestrian Observations*, July 22, 2019, https://pedestrianobservations.com/2019/07/22/new-report-on-construction-costs -misses-the-mark.

But beyond construction, there's a lot we could learn from Europe about what to build and how to operate it.

## From commuter rail to S trains

Many American cities feature a form of transportation known as commuter rail. These are passenger railroad services that run on the mainline tracks of mostly current or former freight railroads but are now geared toward the people who intend to ride into town in the morning and then ride back home in the evening.

These services are generally more expensive to operate than mass transit because they need conductors as well as train drivers, and consequently have higher per mile fares. They also don't run very frequently outside of narrow rush hour windows, and often have no night or weekend service at all. Because of that, they don't really work as all-purpose transportation. People who ride them generally drive their cars just about everywhere, but they park at a suburban train station and then ride downtown for their daily commute—which lets them read or check email during time that would otherwise be spent behind the wheel.

This commuter railroad pattern is a reasonable first attempt at adapting legacy railroad infrastructure to the automobile age. But when the Germans, in the city of Munich, were preparing to host the 1972 Olympic Games, they decided they needed something better. What they did was dig a tunnel between München Hauptbahnhof (Munich Central Station), which served trains entering the city from the west, and München Ost Station, which served trains enter-ing the city from the east. Now commuter trains that entered from the west would run through the tunnel—stopping several times in the city center—and then exit to the east, and trains entering from the east would do the same in the other direction. This created, in effect, a second layer of urban mass transit services that extended out to the suburbs.

They call it the S-Bahn, by analogy with the German term for subway, U-Bahn. And all throughout the German-speaking world, cities that have U-Bahns (Munich, Berlin, Hamburg, Vienna) also have S-Bahns. And even though from a technical standpoint trains running on legacy tracks aren't the same as trains running on iso-lated urban transit networks, the authorities' goal is to make this distinction unimportant to riders. S-Bahn rolling stock is composed of electric multiple units (just like on a subway), so they can acceler-ate rapidly and stop frequently where appropriate. Fares are inte-grated with buses and subways, so you pay the same fare for trips of the same distance regardless of which vehicle you ride. And fare col-lection practices—either gates or random inspections—are identical whether you're on an S-Bahn or a U-Bahn, with free transfers.

Because operating costs are lower, trains can run frequently with low fares. And because the trains run through the city center rather than stopping and turning around, they don't need to wait as long on crowded tracks.

The fact that each route makes *multiple* city center stops also means there isn't such a crush of passengers at any one station, again facilitating faster operations. Higher frequency, cheaper fares, and comprehensive integration with other modes means S-Bahn stations are appropriate locations for transit-oriented development rather than park-and-ride lots. Compared with the American model, the S-Bahn model does require more investment—neither the downtown tunnel nor the electrification of suburban tracks is free—but the investment unlocks incredible value by turning the entire legacy rail network into useful mass transit. The American approach, by contrast, is penny wise and pound foolish—and given some cities' infrastructure plans, it is barely saving money at all.

Munich's S-Bahn is a choice example because it has all the core elements with no additional complications. But a bigger city like Berlin can have multiple central city tunnels. In a smaller city like Leipzig, the S-Bahn isn't a supplemental transportation layer to the U-Bahn—it's the only layer. Zurich, an interesting case, has both multiple central city tunnels and no U-Bahn.

The point is that the basic combination of electrification, simplified fare collection, through-running, and frequent service is a flexible and powerful approach.

The most familiar example to Americans is probably in Paris, where tourists frequently take the RER B to Charles de Gaulle Airport, the RER C to Versailles, or simply find themselves using the central city segments of the RER as a kind of "express" alternative to the Metro. Paris's Châtelet–Les Halles station, between Le Marais and the Louvre, is also a pitch-perfect example of the capacity benefits of modernized operations.

New York officials' current position, for example, is that twenty-one tracks are insufficient to accommodate the volume of demand for trains to Penn Station. But while it's true that most busy commuter train stations around the world have more tracks than that, Châtelet-Les Halles manages more passengers with just seven tracks because the trains enter and leave the station quickly rather than wasting precious center city space for crew changes, brake tests, and other operational slowdowns.

This basic model could greatly improve the transportation systems of several major American cities at modest cost. And while we could make up our own name for it (or copy the French name), because the S-Bahn term is used in many German, Swiss, and Austrian cities, and closely related terms have been adopted in Denmark (S-tog), Italy (S Line), and Czechia (Esko), I think we should just copy it.

Philadelphia, whose commuter trains already run through the center of the city, should adopt modern German-style operational practices and create America's first S train. New York and Washington, DC, already have tracks that run through the center of the city, but do need to invest in some infrastructure upgrades that would actually allow trains to go from Long Island to New Jersey or Virginia to Maryland and vice versa. New York is big enough that if it can get its tunneling costs under control, it would make sense to build more cross-city tunnels—one linking Hoboken Terminal in New Jersey to Atlantic Terminal in Brooklyn via lower Manhattan or even one connecting Grand Central Station to the Staten Island Railroad.*

*For a detailed proposal, see Alon Levy, "How to Get New York Regional Rail Right," *Streetsblog*, January 10, 2018, https://nyc.streetsblog.org/2018/01/10/how-to-get-new-york-regional -rail-right.

Boston would need to invest in electrifying MBTA commuter rail lines, modernizing operational practices, and digging the much-discussed, much-delayed North-South Rail Link. Equivalent ideas could be drawn up for Los Angeles and the Bay Area's Caltrain system. The point in all cases is that upgrading from US-style commuter rail to German-style S trains is a reasonably cheap way to massively upgrade the quality of major American cities' mass transit systems.

Beyond the places with existing rail networks, American cities that are planning transit investments should think harder about the S-train model. At this point quite a few fundamentally car-oriented cities have gone to considerable expense to build nascent light rail systems that generally don't attract many riders. In many cases the Swiss model of building an S train and then incrementally expanding that network could be more attractive. Fundamentally, however, America needs to get back to basics on both roads and trains in terms of understanding what we're trying to accomplish.

## What new stuff is for

To most drivers annoyed by traffic jams, the intuitive answer is to build more or wider highways. The contemporary left tends to critique this notion by invoking the concept of induced demand. The way this works is that the congested state of a highway is a good reason not to drive on it. If you widen the highway and it gets more congested, that encourages more people to live on the farther-out portions of the route, and soon enough the new lanes are filled.

This is true as far as it goes, but it also applies to trains. If a new train reduces congestion on a major highway, it also encourages more people to live on the farther-out stretches of the highway and bring the congestion back.

Fundamentally, only pricing can cure congestion.

But adding capacity does something valuable too—it allows more people to live in more places. And to accommodate one billion Americans, we're going to need to do that, which obviously means more roads and wider ones where reasonable. The key concept of funding road building with user fees and conversion charges is that we *should* build roads that get actual use, but should not be building roads to nowhere. Traffic congestion is a problem, but if you are building new roads that are uncrowded almost all the time, even without a price, you need to ask yourself exactly why you're doing it. An over-crowded bar can be unpleasant, but a bar that's empty all the time is failing.

Meanwhile, trains have a role to play in the automobile age, but it's a fairly specific one. It's a geometrical fact that trains can carry more people through a given volume of space than roads can. That makes trains extremely useful, and the world's biggest and most dynamic cities wouldn't be possible without them. But by the same token, unless trains are frequent and at least sometimes crowded, then they're not serving their purpose.

This speaks to future infrastructure decisions but also critically to housing. The main reason the Los Angeles Metro and other recently built American transit systems underperform on ridership is not enough people live right by the stations. Not-so-gentle density, including tall buildings, elimination of parking and setback minimums, and relief from historical preservation, ought to accompany every train station in America. Outside of New York City few US mass transit lines operate at peak capacity. And even New York has substantial excess capacity in many areas, most notably on the B and C trains on the Upper West Side, in Long Island City, and in large swaths of Brooklyn off of the L train.*

Many new Americans can be accommodated by better using the infrastructure we already have, by funneling people to revitalize cities that have suffered population decline, and by making cost-effective investments to improve capacity at key choke points. But then we should also build new stuff—new stuff that's built precisely with the intention of letting more people live in more places.

It's worth mentioning here that intercity transportation would almost certainly be improved by a larger population.

## Going between cities

The dominance of the media by New York and Washington, DC, often leads to an excessively bleak portrait of America's airport situation. The truth is that according to the Federal Aviation Administration there are only three capacity-constrained airports in the whole country—it just happens that two of them are in New York

---

*Alon Levy, "The Subway in New York is Not at Capacity," *Pedestrian Observations*, February 6, 2018.

and the other is the one members of Congress use to fly home to their districts.

These are important cities, and their airport-crowding issues underscore the fact that investing in high-speed rail, specifically in the Northeast corridor, could be very useful.

But for most Americans the more relevant problem—at least when air service isn't interrupted by a global pandemic—is that the airport they live closest to has only so many direct flights. That means there's little competition on routes, limited flexibility in schedules, and simple logistical difficulties in getting from one place to another. In a day-to-day sense this won't manifest itself as a serious problem because most people rarely fly. But from an economic development standpoint, the fact that midsized cities' connections to the outside world are much worse than what the biggest cities can offer is a major deterrent to growing businesses there.

A bigger country would support a lot more flights. Cities would have more direct connections to more cities. Currently connected city pairs would get more frequent service. More routes would be flown by multiple airlines, bringing competition into the mix. A bigger, thicker national air travel market would mean more connecting options and more flexibility. For residents of virtually every American city it would be a clean win.

And there are fairly simple remedies for the handful of downsides.

Both the Obama and Trump administrations, for example, backed proposals to bring the US Air Traffic Control system into line with global norms by having it run by a nonprofit company separate from the government regulator. That should let us keep more planes in the sky and, in particular, alleviate the capacity crunch around New York City. But as Bart Jansen, *USA Today*'s aviation reporter, explained during the collapse of the most recent legislative push for modernization, "General aviation advocates fear that the corporation will favor airlines at busy airports and will charge higher fees than the government."*

This is true. Compared with the status quo, the reform proposal would prioritize the needs of busy airports over those of "general aviation"—that is, private planes. But that's exactly what we should be doing. Failing to maximize the throughput of the country's most crowded airspace because we're worried that it would raise costs for private plane owners is ridiculous. But it's also broadly typical of the choices we face. The country would be richer and more powerful with more people in it. And the tools are available to fit them into our transportation system. It would mean challenging some stakeholders in the status quo—from private jet owners to contractors getting cushy deals—but it's worth it.

---

*Bart Jansen, "Top House advocate for privatizing air-traffic control drops effort," *USA Today*, February 27, 2018, www.usatoday.com/story/news/2018/02/27/faa-air-traffic-control-privatization/379647002.

## CHAPTER 9

# A Land of Plenty

More transportation infrastructure and a more expansive, family-friendlier welfare state will cost money. And the ability of politicians to sketch out precise schemes to "pay for" their ideas is often taken as a sign of seriousness by the media.

It's worth underscoring that our actual practice is close to the reverse of this. When something is considered genuinely important—typically military funding but often a natural disaster or other crisis (and also tax cuts whenever Republicans are in charge)—Congress simply spends the money. That means a higher budget deficit which could, in principle, lead to high interest rates that create problems for businesses that want to invest or people who want to get mortgages or auto loans. It's been a long time, however, since this problem has manifested itself in practice, so it's probably worth worrying somewhat less about it.

The real challenge of any public spending idea is whether the country actually has the resources and ability to do the job. We can't build a colony on Mars not because we "can't pay for it" but because we literally lack the ability to do it. The government could, by spending huge sums of money, induce a large number of talented scientists and engineers to spend their time working on the problem. But that would be an enormous waste, not so much of money but of talented scientists and engineers. Colonizing Mars would be fun, but it's not clear that it's possible and it doesn't seem to be important. We're better off with technical experts working on building better smartphones, better batteries, better solar panels, better treatments for diseases, and solving other pressing social and commercial problems.

By contrast, there are no hard technical impediments to building more structures that could host day-care facilities or to installing air conditioners in more schools. Hiring and training more staff to safely supervise little kids and to provide older ones with safe and edifying things to do after school and during the summer months is not an entirely trivial problem, and it can't be done overnight. But the country is not running out of able-bodied people who could do this work. Indeed, there is widespread anxiety that automation in the form of self-checkout machines and self-driving cars might lead to mass unemployment of people who lack specialized skills. This worry strikes me as overblown. But at a minimum there's no reason to think we'd be facing a social crisis if a growing child-care and education workforce started pulling labor out of low-wage retail jobs. Most likely the big companies will find technological substitutes. And if they don't, there is clearly no shortage of people living abroad for whom the chance to do low-wage retail work in the United States would be a tremendous opportunity.

All of which is to say that the country clearly can afford, economically speaking, to dedicate more square footage and more person hours of work to caring for and educating children. In the long run, making the required investment might lead to higher interest rates that might require offsets elsewhere. But the most important thing is to focus on the task of actually setting up the new programs in an effective way, not dealing with the accounting issues.

That said, there is much the United States "can afford" simply by virtue of the fact that we are a very rich country. It's reasonable nonetheless for people to worry that substantially increasing our population would leave us poorer on a per person basis. But while concerns about this sort of thing are widespread, they are fundamentally misguided and misunderstand the nature of a modern economy. A larger United States would also be a richer and more vibrant nation.

## How to pay for it

Of course, none of this answers the question of how exactly to finance the programs we need.

One natural place to start is America's existing hodgepodge of confusing and generally regressive child benefits. The 529 savings account program, for example, gives parents a tax break on investment income dedicated to college savings. Some middle-class families use and benefit from this program, but it disproportionately benefits the richest families—those who pay the highest tax rates, have the greatest ability to max out account contributions, and who are most likely to attend high-tuition private colleges. The child and dependent care tax credit is regressive for roughly the same reasons. Head of household tax filing status, likewise, is a useful financial boost to some parents, but it primarily benefits the richest people. All three could be eliminated to partially finance universal benefits.

Those funding sources are, of course, not fully adequate, but they're a start. For paid leave, it's common to see proposals that structure it as a mandate for employers—they simply require them to offer paid leave.

This works well enough, but in practice small employers often end up exempted from mandates, which ends up creating a patchwork system. The FAMILY Act championed by Senator Kirsten Gillibrand and Representative Rosa DeLauro would provide twelve weeks of paid leave for all workers through the Social Security system by imposing a 0.2 percentage point increase in payroll taxes for both employers and employees. This could be structured as a tax imposed on employers with provision to allow the Federal Reserve to automatically suspend the tax as a recession-fighting measure when economic stimulus is needed.

Beyond that, to the extent we need higher taxes, it makes sense to tax things we would like to see less of. One set of popular options involves increasing taxes on the wealthy—either through higher estate taxes, by eliminating the tax-preferred status of investment income, by proposing a new wealth tax, or sometimes simply by raising rates or curbing tax deductions. Tax policy debates can consume endless pages, but the basic logic of all of these ideas is the same. On the one hand, inequality has grown significantly over the past couple of generations. On the other hand, the fundamental premise that the United States is scarce in financial capital and thus needs to fear taxing it excessively appears to no longer be true, if it ever was.

"There are many potential reasons for capital abundance, including the rise of China, changes in the global population structure, the increase in wealth inequality, the increased ease of investing online and so on," explains economist Noah Smith. "But capital abundance also changes the way elected officials, central bankers and economists should think about policy."*

Under contemporary circumstances, transferring resources into an area of genuine scarcity—the care, feeding, clothing, and educating of children—should be a no-brainer. One way to think about this is that even though spending on children codes as "consumption" in conventional economic models, making sure that we have plenty of it is an investment in the future of America in all the relevant senses. That's true in part because more generosity here will directly pay off in terms of better outcomes for children but also in part because making it easier for more families to have more children is an investment in the future of the country.

The other big source of potential tax revenue is taxing bad things. Mark Kleiman, the late New York University drug policy expert,

---

*Noah Smith, "The World Is Awash in Financial Capital," *Bloomberg*, November 13, 2019, www.bloomberg.com/opinion/articles/2019-11-13/world-awash-in-capital-replaces -era-of-scarcity.

estimated that raising the federal alcohol tax to thirty cents a drink would lead to a thousand fewer homicides and two thousand fewer fatal car wrecks per year.* Those are extraordinarily large benefits even before considering all the nonfatal injuries and long-term liver and other health problems that could be ameliorated. The new higher taxes should be indexed to inflation, and the flat tax on alcohol volume should be supplemented by a proportional tax to ensure that well-heeled consumers of high-end stuff pay even more. You could easily raise upward of $100 billion this way over a ten-year time horizon while greatly benefiting public health.

The even bigger target would be carbon dioxide emissions. Emissions taxes to finance investment in children and families are a way of doubly investing in the future of humanity.

Last but by no means least, the United States spends gargantuan sums of money on our military apparatus. Military defense is an important national task, but a very large share of this money seems to be spent on things like prolonged deployments to the Middle East that are only tangentially related to actually defending the country—or even to defending reliable allies. What's more, the very existence of a military with so much capacity for action beyond actual defense needs tends to create demands for further spending. When something bad is happening somewhere in the world—Libya, Syria, wherever—there is often a sense that the United States perhaps ought to "do something" about it. Nobody expects Chile or Singapore to

---

*Reihan Salam, "Alcohol Taxes Should Be Tripled," *Slate*, May 27, 2014, https://slate.com/news-and-politics/2014/05/prohibition-lite-the-war-on-drugs-has-been-a-failure-but-the-war-on-alcohol-deserves-a-second-chance.html.

"do something" about foreign civil wars because there is nothing they can do. But the American military is vast enough that we can, in fact, intervene—albeit at additional cost. If these interventions were systematically helpful, it might be a good reason to maintain such a large defense establishment. But the cost-benefit ratio of trying to help foreigners through military intervention is miserable— indeed, it's difficult to ascertain whether the trillions spent on twenty-first-century wars have been helpful on net at all. By contrast, well-documented public health interventions to fight malaria, worm-born illness, vitamin deficiency, and other relatively straightforward problems could save thousands more lives with millions in additional funding—to say nothing of pandemic preparedness issues that have been endlessly underfunded in favor of "hard" security measures.

Defense spending makes sense if it's needed for defense and not as charity to foreigners. It's uncontroversial in national security circles that the biggest conventional military challenge to the United States stems from China. And investing in ensuring that the United States can deter China and contribute meaningfully to the defense of allies in the Asia-Pacific region is perfectly reasonable. But as Chinese national strength over the long term stems fundamentally from its huge scale, money spent at the margin on growing the national population will be money well spent.

Last but by no means least, it really is worth emphasizing that at least under present economic conditions there's no particular immediate need to worry about financing details or the budget deficit. Both interest rates and inflation have been low for years, and while that might change in the future, it's not an immediate problem. Indeed, the low interest rates themselves are arguably a problem that more population growth could solve.

## Beating secular stagnation

In the late 1930s, economist Alvin Hansen postulated that the American economy had entered a period of what he called secular stagnation, in which only large sustained budget deficits could prevent a recurrence of the kind of mass unemployment experienced during the Great Depression.[*]

World War II delivered the deficits Hansen called for, and during the postwar demobilization period there was some concern that he might be right—though the next several decades clearly proved him wrong.

More recently, however, former treasury secretary Larry Summers revived the concept after noting that ever since the 2008 financial crisis, major world economies have paired ultralow interest rates with soaring budget deficits and complacent inflation. The issue, as he describes it, is "an imbalance resulting from an increasing propensity to save and a decreasing propensity to invest."

There is, in other words, too much cash sloshing around the world's financial system and not enough real investment in pro-

---

[*]Alvin Hansen, "Economic Progress and Declining Population Growth," *American Economic Review*, March 1939: 1-15.

ductive enterprises. Consequently, "When significant growth is achieved . . . it comes from dangerous levels of borrowing that translate excess savings into unsustainable levels of investment"— financial bubbles, in other words.*

On the one hand, this is an opportunity to run big budget deficits without worrying too much about it (essentially the Trump administration's approach). But on the other hand, it does pose some worrying questions about economic stability. For starters, our normal time-tested way of fighting recessions is to ask the Federal Reserve to cut interest rates. This worked very well for years, but it ran into trouble in 2008–2009 when they cut rates all the way down to zero and that still wasn't enough. Then, over a decade later, with the unemployment rate low, interest rates were still at what would have traditionally been considered emergency levels. That meant that when the coronavirus pushed the global economy back into recession, there was only so much room to respond with rate cuts—raising the risk that high unemployment will persist even once the public health emergency passes.

Population growth does not figure that centrally in Summers's writing on secular stagnation, but it was at the heart of Hansen's original analysis.

The *American Economic Review* paper in which Hansen outlined it—and the earlier 1938 talk on which the paper was based—was titled "Economic Progress and Declining Population Growth," and

---

*Larry Summers, "The Age of Secular Stagnation," *Foreign Affairs*, February 15, 2016, http://larrysummers.com/2016/02/17/the-age-of-secular-stagnation.

was founded on the basic observation that investment volume is on some level a function of the projected future population. If you expect many more people to be around twenty years from now, then it makes sense to engage in a lot of costly capital-intensive investments—building new homes for them to live in, new stores for them to shop in, new offices for them to work in, and the industrial capacity necessary to construct all that stuff. The big reason Hansen's forecast turned out to be wrong is that the conclusion of World War II led to the Baby Boom. Hansen's premise was that policy makers had to think harder about the macroeconomics of slow population growth. But population growth sped up, so there was nothing to think about.

Today, though, Hansen's demographic forecasts are coming true and giving his economic analysis new relevance. In spring 2020, interest rates are lower in Japan than in the European Union and lower in the EU than in the United States. It's not a coincidence that America has faster population growth than Europe and that Japan's is even lower. Australia, whose population is growing faster than America's, largely thanks to immigration, has had the highest rates in the developed world for most of the twenty-first century. With population robust, there's plenty of market demand for tangible investments.

This is all incredibly far removed from normal people's political or economic concerns. But the problem with interest rates that are very low even when the unemployment rate is low is that it leaves governments unable to deploy their traditional recession-fighting tool—interest rate cuts—when the unemployment rate starts to rise. A faster-growing population would lead to higher interest rates during good times, allowing rate cuts to be deployed during bad times to stabilize the economy.

That's just one more reason to think a population growth agenda would lead to a richer country, and thus that we can surely afford to make the investments necessary to achieve it—especially because America has more than enough natural resources to support a much larger population.

## We have the resources we need

Oftentimes in life, myths grow up to justify elements of the status quo that simply reflect policy choices. Many New Yorkers, for example, are taught to believe that something about the geological structure of Manhattan makes it impossible to build skyscrapers between the financial district and Midtown. This is completely untrue—rents were too low there to justify skyscraper construction for most of the twentieth century, and now that rents are higher, the modern zoning code doesn't allow it.*

By the same token, when I discuss the basic facts of comparative population density with people, they tend to reach for deep explanations rooted in ecology and natural resources to explain why America is less densely populated than the developed countries of Europe and Asia.

---

*Alissa Walker, "Five Myths About New York City Skyscrapers Debunked," *Curbed*, October 6, 2016, https://ny.curbed.com/2016/10/6/13189862/nyc-skyscrapers-myths-jason-barr.

Perhaps our country is too arid, for example?

But America turns out to have 8,800 cubic meters of fresh water per person. If our population tripled, we would have 2,900—quite a bit less. Yet Spain gets by with 2,400; the UK has 2,200; Germany has 1,300; and the Netherlands has 650. Qatar, an admittedly extreme case, gets by with fewer than 25 cubic meters. For the United States to make itself as parched as Qatar seems inadvisable, but we'd need a population of 112 billion, which is obviously a bit extreme.

The point, however, is that even Qatar is able to provide people with drinking water.

What is true, of course, is that they are not growing a lot of food in Qatar. The United States, by contrast, is a farming powerhouse that leads the world in gross exports of agricultural commodities. If our population tripled, this would probably change in the sense that a larger share of our massive farm bounty would be consumed at home rather than shipped abroad in exchange for Asian manufactured goods. But that's simply to say that America generates massive surpluses of food and can easily accommodate more eaters.

Indeed even as the total acreage of American farms has steadily shrunk since World War II, total farm output has nearly tripled thanks to improved efficiency.* And that's occurring in a context where there's been relatively little reason to truly focus on maximizing what can be squeezed out of the land. Over in Europe, the very

---

*U.S. Department of Agriculture, *Farming and Farm Income*, September 2018, www.ers .usda.gov/data-products/ag-and-food-statistics-charting-the-essentials/farming-and-farm -income.

densely populated Netherlands has turned itself into a high-tech farming powerhouse that produces 5 percent of the European Union's total agricultural income while having way less than 1 percent of the land.* The story of exactly how it pulled this off is complicated but, essentially it involves switching to a model of farming that uses more capital and land. Profiling Dutch farming for *National Geographic*, for example, Frank Viviano reports on a farm for leafy greens where "each acre in the greenhouse yields as much lettuce as 10 outdoor acres and cuts the need for chemicals by 97 percent."[†]

The point is not to prescribe a specific agricultural policy for the future, or to deny that conflicts exist over the best use of water in specific places.

The point is simply that just as a country of one billion Americans would not be particularly crowded by European or Asian standards, is also wouldn't be particularly parched or short of farmland. The United States has been a relatively sparsely populated country for the entirety of its existence, and has risen to power and prominence in the world by deliberately fostering an above-average population growth rate. We have sound geopolitical and economic reasons to want to return to relatively fast population growth, and nothing about the fundamentals on the resources side has changed—America has plenty of just about everything.

---

*Eurostat, "Agriculture in the European Union and the Member States—Factsheets," www .ec.europa.eu/agriculture/statistics/factsheets_en.

†Frank Viviano, "This Tiny Country Feeds the World," *National Geographic*, September 2007.

## There's room for nature too

I am not personally a nature lover or an outdoorsy person, but for those who are it's worth emphasizing that an expanded population need not come at the expense of wilderness or outdoor recreations.

The vast majority of the actual land that we need to accommodate a larger population is present in the already settled areas of the country. We have shrunken cities that can be repopulated. And most of those cities have industrial and transportation logistics facilities that are no longer needed and can be converted to residential uses. Most of our thriving and growing metropolitan areas are not especially dense and in fact feature draconian regulatory policies to prevent single-family detached homes from being replaced with apartments. Online shopping, meanwhile, is putting pressure on many forms of traditional retailing and opening up further possibilities for converting already developed land into housing.

Something many people don't appreciate is that America's public lands are vast, but for the most part are not actually used for conservation purposes. The federal government owns about 28 percent of all the land in the United States. The military has its own vast tracts of land, but only about an eighth of civilian federal acreage—less than 4 percent of the country as a whole—is under the stewardship of the National Park Service.

The vast majority of the rest is run by various arms of the Department of the Interior and the Department of Agriculture, which allow grazing, forestry, or other forms of natural resource preservation and extraction on their territory.

This is not by any means necessarily a bad idea—a country needs mines and lumber. But this, rather than urban housing, is where the proximate conflicts around nature conservation arise. Typically, Democratic Party presidents use the broad authority granted under the Antiquities Act to shift various parcels of federal land. This is usually opposed by Republicans, who believe that allowing for continued exploitation by the logging and mining industries would be a better use of land. Reasonable people can disagree about some of the specific cases here. But it's worth understanding that the actual conflict is whether uninhabited land should be used for parks or for resource-extraction industries—the growth of human settlement isn't really the issue.

Indeed, even when we're not talking about federal land, the same basic conflict between park uses and industry tends to rear its head. Consider the years of effort by conservationists to create a North Maine Woods National Park out of some of the several million acres of forest land currently owned primarily by timber companies. This is land that largely lacks towns or paved roads and that, by tradition, is available for camping, hunting, and fishing even as parts of the vast forest are periodically clear-cut. The idea of turning this into a park has long been championed by liberals in southern Maine and by visitors who love the state, but it's generally resisted by people who live near the hypothetical park and who don't want to give up on the possibility of a general revival in the logging industry.

This debate is unlikely to be resolved soon. Meanwhile, the actual towns in the area—Patten, Greenville, Sherman—and, indeed, Piscataquis and Aroostook Counties, are losing population. There is plenty of space for more people in the populated areas whether or not we build the park—it's the same situation that applies to conflicts about the disposition of federal land in the West.

The billion Americans proposal is radical enough that it's best to stay agnostic on other issues. Suffice it to say, tripling the population would not prevent us from expanding parkland and wildlife preservation were we to decide those are important priorities.

# A hotter world

The one resource I'm not confidently blasé about is the atmosphere's ability to continue absorbing greenhouse gas emissions without unleashing catastrophic effects on global weather problems.

The most alarmist voices have created a somewhat unnecessary sense of panic about this issue in some people's minds, but the bigger picture is that world governments continue to underreact considerably relative to the scale of the threat. But properly understood, climate change isn't a big impediment to the vision of one billion Americans in large part because the problem remains so daunting under current policy.

A larger population does mean somewhat higher $CO_2$ emissions for a variety of reasons. But in terms of meeting the multifaceted challenge of climate change, the billion Americans agenda isn't a big deal. There are parts of climate policy that are substantively easy but politically challenging, and a bigger population doesn't make them any more challenging. Then there are parts of climate policy that involve difficult technical problems, and a bigger population doesn't make them any more challenging either. Last but by no means least, there is the considerable question of how to help the world adapt to the reality of rising temperatures, where the billion Americans agenda mostly serves to help.

Finally, it's worth dwelling on the international aspect of the climate problem that tends to get downplayed in US progressive circles only to be overemphasized by outright denialisms on the right. The key point here, however, is that the United States does not hold the fate of global atmospheric conditions solely in its hands. Chinese greenhouse gas emissions are double ours at this point. And while we are still putting out about two times as much carbon dioxide as India, our emissions are falling even under Trump, while India's are rising rapidly. And under current conditions, if other large poor countries like Nigeria, Bangladesh, and Indonesia manage to experience rapid growth, their emissions will soar too.

"Most people in these countries have living standards that are a fraction of ours," writes Kevin Drum. "And they justifiably ask why they should cut back on energy consumption and consign themselves to poverty . . . this is the hinge point on which the future of climate change rests."*

---

*Kevin Drum, "We Need a Massive Climate War Effort—Now," *Mother Jones*, January/February 2020, www.motherjones.com/politics/2019/12/kevin-drum-climate-change-reseach.

This shouldn't be seen as an excuse for inaction. But it's a reason to see that minimizing US greenhouse gas emissions can't be the be-all and end-all of climate policy. To maximize our contribution to a very serious problem, we need to maximize our contribution to a *global* solution by first inventing and then deploying the means necessary to make high living standards sustainable. The resources we lack are primarily political will and technical innovations to solve thorny problems. A bigger denser country will be better situated to contribute the ideas and inventions that can solve the problem. And a strong, powerful, and confident United States is much more likely to lead the world to the kind of global cooperation that is needed than is a suspicious, inward-looking, declining America locked in to peer competition with the rising powers of Asia.

# Epilogue

## We the (Not Enough) People

It's customary when trying to talk Americans into daunting political problems to quote JFK on the subject of why go to the Moon.

"We choose to go to the moon," he said. "We choose to go to the moon in this decade and do the other things, not because they are easy, but because they are hard, because that goal will serve to organize and measure the best of our energies and skills, because that challenge is one that we are willing to accept, one we are unwilling to postpone, and one which we intend to win, and the others, too."*

It's a great speech. That being said, it's worth emphasizing that while one billion Americans may be impossible and absurd, there's actually nothing *hard* about it.

---

*John F. Kennedy, "Moon Speech," Rice University, September 12, 1962, https://er.jsc.nasa.gov/seh/ricetalk.htm.

Letting more hardworking and talented foreign-born people move here is not hard. On the contrary, it's keeping people out that's hard. Providing financial support so that Americans can have as many children as they say they'd like to is a big change, but there's nothing particularly difficult about it. Letting builders make whatever kind of housing their customers want to buy is easy. Shifting economic activity to places where land and buildings are cheap is a little more difficult, but it's hardly a voyage to the moon. Copying a traffic-management paradigm that Singapore implemented in the mid-1970s isn't hard at all, nor is copying long-standing German commuter rail practices.

These easy things feel hard because we've become accustomed to a political culture that can barely do anything at all. One view is that we as a nation ought to constrain our ambitions to fit the contours of our depressing politics. A more optimistic view might be that a renewed political focus on the big questions—economic growth, international competition, and the future of the American project— might help heal a political system that seems currently trapped by internecine conflict.

Large, complicated organizations often benefit from having a mission statement written down so that the diverse stakeholders involved in making day-to-day decisions can periodically orient their thinking to appropriate ends.

The United States of America is fortunate to have a couple. Our Declaration of Independence states that all men are created equal, and our Constitution clarifies that its goals are to "provide for the common defence, promote the general Welfare, and secure the Blessings of Liberty to ourselves and our Posterity."

Neither document tells us *how* to accomplish those things. That's what politics is for. But it's helpful to be reminded time and again that that *really* is what politics is for—not for special interests to try to enrich themselves or for politicians to enact proxy battles over symbolic disputes in national or global culture.

How can we secure the blessings of liberty to ourselves and our posterity? In its early days, the United States was a fairly weak country subject to the imperial machinations of England and France. But our leaders deliberately built a stronger country. They encouraged the growth of domestic industry with tariffs but also with canals and railroads. And they encouraged the growth of the population. Aspects of immigration have always been controversial and probably always will be. But early American leaders fundamentally did not worry that more people would mean less land to go around. They worried that without more people the land would not be developed to its fullest potential, and the country's growth would be stymied.

Then for a long time, we didn't need to worry much about such things.

The key question of the twentieth century was not whether the United States would be the most powerful nation in the world, but what we would do with that power. In Europe, in Asia, and often in Latin America and Africa as well the question of what would the United States do (or not do) was very frequently the critical issue in world affairs.

But American preeminence was always built on two foundations. On the one hand, we were much bigger than the other rich countries. On the other hand, we were much richer than the other big countries. Today, we are still much richer than the countries with larger populations than ours. But the gap has narrowed. And it seems likely to further narrow. We should do what we can to make our country rich, but realistically it is hard for countries that are already rich to grow faster than countries that are catching up. We can hope that our rivals stumble, but hope is not a plan, and keeping foreigners mired in poverty forever would not be a very good plan anyway.

The alternative is to think bigger. The prospect of more rapid population growth raises lots of concerns, problems, and fears, and I've done my best to give plausible responses to them. If other people have better ideas or just different preferences about the details, then more power to them.

But let's have this conversation.

Let's secure the blessings of liberty to ourselves and our posterity.

# Acknowledgments

The world went through some incredibly dramatic upheavals during the relatively brief span of time that I worked on this book, a period during which it has been a tremendous privilege to be in a line of work that can be pursued effectively from the safety of a bedroom or a basement. Under the circumstances, my thoughts and thanks in the first instance go to the millions of Americans who are not so privileged and who spent their time on the front lines— delivering health care, keeping the food system and the retail economy running, driving the buses, and otherwise holding the country together during a mind-boggling failure of national leadership.

More prosaically, this book simply would not exist without my agent, Matt Carlini from Javelin, who roused me from a creative torpor and got me thinking bigger, or without Dana Treistman, who encouraged me to worry less and do more.

## ACKNOWLEDGMENTS

Adrian Zackheim at Portfolio inspired me with his own enthusiasm for the pitch and with his eagerness to get the project executed. Trish Daly, my editor, saved me from more than one blunder, as did my good friend Rachael Brown, a super fact-checker.

I have always felt that copyediting my typo-challenged drafts is one of the most challenging jobs in the world, and I owe a debt to Susan Johnson for shouldering it and to Christina Caruccio and Lisa Thornbloom for proofreading. Beyond the words themselves, there is a whole fantastic team behind the design, production, marketing, and publicity of a book, and the coordination of all the moving parts. So many thanks to Ryan Boyle, Caitlin Noonan, Jessica Regione, Jen Heuer, Meighan Cavanaugh, Niki Papadopoulos, Nina Rodriguez-Marty, Tara Gilbride, Margot Stamas, Amanda Lang, Jamie Lescht, and Nicole McArdle for all of their hard work.

Remaining errors and shortcomings are, of course, my own.

I'm privileged to work in my day job at *Vox*, pound for pound the greatest powerhouse of ideas journalism in the galaxy. The team of editors I work with there—Laura McGann, Kay Steiger, Libby Nelson, Elbert Ventura, Caroline Houck, and Sean Collins—are brilliant and tireless. Most, if not all, of the ideas in this book got workshopped in some form as articles that they edited. My cohosts on *The Weeds* podcast, Dara Lind and Jane Coaston, are witty and incisive and always inspire me to raise my game in an effort to keep up with them. Jeff Geld, our producer, keeps me sane and unwittingly helped me orchestrate some interviews that were integral to the coming together of the book. Ezra Klein and Melissa Bell, my cofounders at *Vox*, never fail to call me on my bullshit when needed and are the ultimate advocates of thinking bigger—I always try to reach the standard they set for ambition and execution.

Beyond my two workplaces, I rely, of course, on an informal brain trust. My old friends Brian Beutler, Kriston Capps, David Montes, Sam Rosenfeld, Daniel Schlozman, and Jeff Theodore counsel me through everything. The guys in the dads group chat keep me sane.

Outside of close friends, I want to pay a special homage to Laura Foote, Brian Hanlon, and other leaders of the California YIMBY movement whose work is not only making the world a better place, but who really convinced me that ideas do matter.

Speaking of ideas, there is little that is genuinely original in the book and everyone from whom I've borrowed on specific points should be recognized in the text or in the footnotes. But the book owes a vast inspirational debt to the Canadian journalist Doug Saunders and his book *Maximum Canada*. In tweet form, this whole book is simply "*Maximum Canada*, but for America." Speaking of Twitter, while the platform has had in some ways a corrosive influence on the public dialogue, it's proven to me in other respects to be an invaluable means of making connections with a wide-ranging group of scholars and activists. Likely none of them agree with the hodgepodge synthesis I've made of their ideas to assemble my thesis, but I am grateful every day for everyone who takes the time to engage in public service and public education for free on the internet.

Finally my wife, Kate, keeps it real in terms of what people actually want to read and kept me on track innumerable times during this project when I was ready to give up or get mad. Without her, I'm nothing.